Samuel Gompers
and
Organized Labor
in America

Harold C. Livesay

Samuel Gompers
and
Organized Labor
in America

WAVELAND

PRESS, INC.

Prospect Heights, Illinois

Frontispiece courtesy of the AFL–CIO.

For information about this book, write or call:

Waveland Press, Inc.
P.O. Box 400
Prospect Heights, Illinois 60070
(708) 634-0081

Printed in the United States of America

7   6   5   4   3

Dedication

THIS BOOK is joyously dedicated to the most gorgeous assortment of characters I ever knew — Dirty Neck Jones and Sweet Pea Wilson, Good Gerry Gregg and Bad Charley Bromwell, Air Force Jones and Pink Pajamas Horner, Senator Ellingsworth and Blondie McCardle, Dizzy Doermann and Mutt Lutton, Bullet Wingate and Lead Shoes Cullen, Johnny Tomatoes and Johnny Bananas, Pancho Gonzales and Studs Bero, Ryan and Mulrooney, Savinski and Trusczinski, Collella and Tenaglia, and all the other rollickers, grousers, hard workers, and featherbedders I railroaded with for ten years. Good guys and bad, friends and enemies, career men and vagabonds, in locomotive cabs, cabooses, yard offices, and all-night diners, they taught me a trade. They taught me something else too: that the real repository of America's tradition of individualism is out there in those "toiling masses," not in the companies that pay them but can't buy them, not in the unions that represent them but don't speak for them, and not in the minds of those who study them but rarely understand them.

Editor's Preface

A PROFOUND AMBIGUITY long hobbled all attempts to organize workingmen in the United States. Through much of the nineteenth century, wage earners who sought to unite in defense of their interests could not be sure who in the labor force was in a position to join a unified movement. As a result, false starts, internal dissension, and sectarian conflict were commonplace; and many a hopeful start ran only into a dead end.

Several factors contributed to the uncertainty about the character of the American labor movement. The initial efforts came while industry was still primitive, operated by independent handicraftsmen. Indeed, the first stirrings of self defense emanated from skilled artisans, many of whom were self-employed and some of whom were, in fact, the masters of other workers. Even when mechanization altered the situation, class lines in the United States remained less stable than in other countries so that the proletariat did not feel a sense of solidarity or act as if it were conscious of its own group identity.

Furthermore, many pioneer labor leaders espoused objectives broader than those of the group they sought to mobilize and aimed not simply to improve wages and conditions of work but also to reform the whole society. Since social mobility and the frontier enabled many Americans to move away from the places and status of their birth, it was tempting to set goals which would help people get out of less desirable jobs and into more desirable ones rather than just to lighten their toil. The first important workingmen's party, for instance, dedicated itself to making western lands and public education universally available. Hence intellectuals, reformers, and politicians found this an attractive field of agitation, though their aims were rarely the same as those of the workers.

By the end of the nineteenth century, massive industrialization and large scale immigration had further complicated the situation. Drawn from diverse ethnic backgrounds, the vast armies of labor who manned the great new mills and factories found little relevance to their plight in the ideals and programs of the past. Nor did they respond to the ideologically motivated preachers of various socialist doctrines.

It was the particular talent of Samuel Gompers to have perceived the realities of the position of working people in the United States. He was one of them himself. Pragmatically, he developed a pattern of action and a philosophy which enabled one segment of the labor force to organize itself effectively. Those who joined his American Federation of Labor were largely skilled workers; the great mass of industrial employees was still unorganized when Gompers died. Nevertheless, the forms he outlined and the procedures he followed later in the twentieth century provided the basis for the ultimate formation of a powerful American labor movement.

Professor Livesay's thoughtful book clarifies the main forces that operated not only in the life of the colorful figure who is its central subject but also in the economic and social background against which Samuel Gompers acted.

OSCAR HANDLIN

Contents

Samuel Gompers
and
Organized Labor
in America

I
Learning an Old Trade and Finding a New Home
1850–1869

To MOST AMERICANS the term "organized labor" means the American Federation of Labor and its associate, the Congress of Industrial Organizations. Though often damned as too weak by its members, or as too strong by business, press, and public, the AFL–CIO enjoys general recognition as a permanent, powerful force. Politicians woo its support and investigate its behavior. Business negotiates with its affiliates, acknowledges its legitimacy, and respects its strength. Presidents consult with its leaders and enlist its participation in government. The American economy, once regarded as the province of unfettered business, is now accepted as a partnership among big business, big government, and big labor.

Labor's place in this triumvirate is of recent vintage, only achieved during the Great Depression of the 1930s. Before then the unions' struggle was for survival, not for parity. The fact that organized labor as it exists in the late twentieth century is largely the product of the AF of L and its leaders obscures the federation's recent and inauspicious beginnings. What became the keystone of the modern American labor movement emerged from a tiny conclave of skilled tradesmen who met in Columbus, Ohio, in 1886 and founded the American Federation of Labor.

In its first years, the federation gave little hint of its potent future role. The organization and its president, Samuel Gompers, a cigarmaker by trade, seemed unlikely saviors for the American worker. Indeed, they more resembled a storefront church, small in membership, fervent in creed, but no more likely to become the universal faith than any of its rivals, despite the visionary intentions of its founders. They designed the AF of L as an agency to coordinate the activities of existing craft unions throughout the United States and to create new organizations where necessary. These pioneers hoped to unite the laborers of America under the trade-union banner and lead them to dignity and prosperity.

These were ambitious goals, particularly in the light of past experience and current circumstances. Although workers' organizations in one form or another had been around since colonial times, they had repeatedly succumbed to business depressions, internal bickering, and political Pied Pipers. In 1886 they faced a task multiplied by the emergence of huge industrial units, far more powerful antagonists than the small, individually operated firms of the past. Whether the craft union, or a national organization of craft unions for that matter, could prosper in the new environment remained to be seen. The omens were not auspicious; indeed, the first act of Gompers and his fellows at Columbus, before launching a new national organization, was to scuttle an unsuccessful predecessor.

And there was no guarantee that the AF of L would attract many workers. Competitors existed in plenty, with other unions as well as political parties contending for the role of labor's champion by offering a variety of reform programs. Compared to the utopian visions and flamboyant rhetoric of its rivals, the AF of L's plan seemed modest. Gompers and his cohorts agreed to bar nonworkers entirely and to concentrate on the skilled first. They thought labor could achieve all it wanted in society by staying out of politics, avoiding reform movements, and sticking to strikes and boycotts.

At the time of its birth, few people thought much of the AF of L's chances. Gompers believed otherwise, and time proved him right. One by one the rivals died while the AF of L lived on. Many reasons accounted for its longevity, but foremost was the shrewd perception of its founders. Gompers saw as few others did that in America labor must shape itself to the contours of its society rather than try to remake society. He realized that American workers endorsed principles that they carried with them everywhere, even to work. Donning overalls wrought no magic transformation of the multifaceted work force into a single-minded body. To succeed, any labor movement would have to take the workers as they came, accept their principles, and weave them into a whole fabric.

These principles included pursuing personal independence to the point of perversity. Americans did not like to be rounded up, even for their own good. That they sometimes had to submit to organization and discipline — as in the factory — made them all the less agreeable to it in labor organizations and the like where such compliance remained voluntary. In nursing the AF of L from birth to maturity, Gompers had to find a way to coax collective action out of a motley of dedicated individualists.

This dedication to independence and free will, transplanted by the colonists, swiftly took root in the soil of North America. On a continent so vast, land holding, restricted in England to the fortunate few, was possible for any free man bold enough to strike out on his own. The availability of land thus encouraged individualism. These characteristics, once a hallmark of the aristocracy, soon permeated all levels of society and became a tradition as cherished as social mobility, and as tightly linked to the rights of private property.

The waves of immigrants that flooded the land in the nineteenth and early twentieth centuries intensified the American obsession with individualism. Courageous and self-reliant, the immigrants persuaded themselves that they had found a better life justifying the toil and sacrifice required to survive in the New World; moreover, they inculcated the ideals of free will, property, and social mobility into their children, thus nurturing these traditions as vigorously as the native-born.

The country's evolution — from a colonial society in which many were self-sufficient or nearly so into a modern industrial society in which everyone relied constantly on the services of others — subjected traditional beliefs to massive strains. Furthermore, the United States' enormous material progress, achieved through rapid industrialization, the factory system, and the division of labor into assembly-line jobs, magnified and accelerated those strains within the workplace.

During this period of momentous change in the methods of production, Samuel Gompers grew to maturity and rose to the leadership of the American labor movement's first viable national organization. The story of Gompers and the AF of L is the story of a minority (the organized workers) of the work force, itself a minority within the whole population. Viewed in historical perspective, however, the theories, goals, and methods of Gompers and his associates, together with the successes and failures of the AF of L, show how Americans tried to preserve their traditional ideals in the shifting maelstrom of the industrial workplace.

The story also reveals how the ideals themselves dictated the strategies designed to preserve them. During the last third of the nineteenth century, an industrial economy threatened to transform individualistic, ambitious, property-oriented craftsmen into a depersonalized, impoverished, permanent working class of unskilled machine-tenders. The working men responded to the unsettling present and prepared for the ominous future in terms that squared with ideals rooted in the past. Believing in individualism, they supported only organizations that demanded little sacrifice of personal autonomy; subscribing to social mobility, they rejected theories that required acceptance of a permanent working-class status for themselves and their children; owning property (or aspiring to do so), they declined to work for property's abolition; accepting the rule of law, they repudiated lawlessness; trusting in democracy and enjoying the vote, they opposed violent overthrow of the government; embracing the concept of general welfare, they spurned tactics that might impede the forward movement of society as a whole. As pragmatists they found little appeal in movements that did not offer immediate results.

American workers thus rejected many methods resorted to by Europeans, such as the formation of revolutionary labor parties, participation in general strikes, agitation for public ownership of the means of production, and machine breaking. No labor organization that espoused such methods ever lasted long in the United States. The AF of L endured not because it had a blueprint for a new world, or for a return to an old one, but because it best managed to protect the cherished rights of its members against the inroads of the new industrial age. Gompers and his brethren never asked the workers to abandon their beliefs in order to protect their rights. The AF of L limited itself to economic and political methods sanctioned by the prevailing system. In this it reflected the outlook of its chief, for Gompers translated his own understanding of America into labor policies and forced them on the organization whenever he could.

Gompers's life passed through several periods. First there was his boyhood and young manhood in England and America. Until he was nineteen, he was absorbed in the lessons of the streets and the classroom, in learning and practicing his trade as a cigarmaker, and in making a home for himself and his family. Union affairs concerned him little more than the social clubs to which he belonged. In fact, his interest in the cigarmakers' union derived more from its fraternal benefits than from its economic functions.

At the age of nineteen he entered a period of transition in outlook and of growth to leadership, a process triggered by

changing economic conditions that threatened extinction of
his trade. Gompers injected himself into his union's affairs.
Finding the union inadequate to protect the membership
against mechanization and hostile employers, he and a handful of allies created a new union local, structured internally
like the British trade unions Gompers had observed in his
youth, but employing a practical policy of strikes, boycotts,
and negotiations to meet the imperatives of the American
environment. When this plan succeeded, Gompers and his
friends then remade the cigarmakers' national union in the
image of their local.

Building on the lessons learned while organizing his own
craft, Gompers grew to aggressive maturity, which lasted
through the First World War. During this time, he and like-
minded trade unionists sought to establish a national federation of craft organizations. This campaign culminated in the
founding of the AF of L in 1886 and in Gompers's election to
its presidency. In the decade and a half that followed, he
pursued offensive strategies, hoping to gather the entire American work force into trade unions affiliated with the AF of L.
Simultaneously, he struggled to defend the federation against
its enemies, including rival unions, socialists, political sooth-
sayers, business, and government.

As the first decade of the twentieth century unfolded, Gompers passed from aggressive maturity into a defensive middle
age. Beset by crippling attacks on many sides, he relinquished
hope of organizing all workers and concentrated on preserving
the skilled trades unions that formed the backbone of the
AF of L. This defensive battle, waged on picket lines, at negotiating tables, in the courts and legislative halls, and in the
drawing rooms of financiers and industrialists, seemed to cul-
minate in victory with the election of Woodrow Wilson, the
passage of progressive reforms, and the brief interlude of
favored status enjoyed by labor during the First World War.

With peace, however, came disappointment: for the man,
an enfeebled, embittered old age; for the organization, re-

verses that swept away many hard-won gains. By the time Gompers died in 1924, the AF of L had become moribund. Gompers's ultimate achievement thus lay not in building a mass labor movement, for that he never did, but in creating a viable (albeit an elitist) national federation of skilled trades unions that made solid gains for their members.

His failures and successes had a common root in his determination to operate within the mainstream of American society. In effect, this meant that unions survived only where the public would tolerate them, in the small shops and in artisan trades where craft unions seemed to uphold American individualistic values, but not in large industries, where labor organizations seemed — to many trade-union leaders, to the public, and to business — to threaten the same code. Although he worked hard to allay such fears, Gompers succeeded only partially. He converted few colleagues to the cause of organizing the unskilled because most leaders thought such a program would destroy their unions and deprive the skilled workers of their higher status and better wages.

Gompers repudiated socialism, accepted industrialization, embraced big business, and tried to persuade the public that organized labor was a respectable, responsible component of the American establishment. He never convinced the majority, however, that organization of the mass of industrial workers did not threaten the country with socialism or communism.

Most industrialists rejected his conciliatory suggestions that business and unions had a common interest, and that bargaining with workers made more sense than fighting them. The public's hostility to industrial unions helped big business repeal the AF of L's more aggressive assaults with brutal anti-labor tactics justified to the people, to the legislatures, and to the courts as necessary to defend the sacred American free-enterprise system against a mortal enemy.

Whenever his plans threatened to shatter the AF of L, or whenever his opponents succeeded in branding his methods as un-American or illegal, Gompers, dedicated to union solidarity, committed to American ideals and convinced that labor must operate within them, saw no choice but to retreat to safer ground and await a more opportune moment.

The moment did not come in his lifetime. Gompers left the trade-union movement essentially where he found it — in the small shop and craft industries. He left it better paid, working shorter hours, more strongly organized, but little broader in scope. Adherence to the prevailing system of values permitted his organization to survive and grow to a certain point, while bringing real benefits to its membership. The same values prevented the AF of L from expanding into the modern industrial sector and from giving similar advantages to the great mass of workers who labored there. For his inability to overcome this limitation, Gompers suffered much criticism, both during his life and after. He made his share of mistakes, but fewer than his predecessors or his rivals. In his time he built as best he could on the territory he could hold. His successors have done no more.

Like so many Americans prominent in the country's history, Samuel Gompers was an immigrant. Born in London in 1850, he emigrated to New York with his family in 1863. His response to his new surroundings reflected views developed during his boyhood. His outlook, however, was not typically British, for his parents had themselves emigrated from Holland before Sam was born, and in many ways they remained more Dutch than English. Sam sailed for America with a mixture of traditional attitudes inculcated by his Dutch-Jewish family and by the Jewish free school he attended for four years, attitudes tempered by the informal education he acquired in the narrow streets and sweaty workshops of East London.

The Gompers family was extensive, with branches scattered across Europe. Some of Sam's ancestors and relatives distinguished themselves as scholars, poets, mathematicians, composers, and businessmen. Both his grandfathers prospered as merchants; the paternal one, Samuel (for whom Sam was named), followed his elder brother to England in 1845 and established an import-export business. Sam's father, Solomon, however, entered the family's other traditional occupation, cigarmaking, a craft long practiced in Holland and engaged in by many of Sam's uncles and cousins.

As a Dutchman, a Jew, and a workingman, Solomon Gompers and his family never became part of England, however long they remained in it. The momentous events of Victorian England — the building of the Empire, the struggle for power between the traditional landed gentry and the emerging class of wealthy industrialists, the battles for electoral reforms and for reforms in sanitation, in the factory, and elsewhere — all these took place in a world far removed from the one in which the Gompers lived. For them the halls of Parliament and the fields of India were equally distant.

Whatever the English traditions of liberty and law meant to Englishmen themselves, particularly those fortunate enough to be wellborn or wealthy, they had little immediate impact on the lives of impoverished workers. England had long been a sanctuary for refugees from political repression, wars, and pogroms in Europe. (The most illustrious of them, Karl Marx, arrived the year before Sam was born.) But it had never since Norman times attracted many immigrants from outside the United Kingdom. Even London itself, the seat of the Empire, the world's largest metropolis, the nexus of global trade and finance, had a population that was 98 percent British as late as 1880.

Within the tiny fraction of London's populace that was foreign-born, Jews suffered an additional disability. Mid-nineteenth-century British society discriminated against even wealthy, native-born Jews. When Baron Rothschild was elected to the House of Lords by the City of London in 1847, he was refused his seat because he declined to swear the parliamentary oath, required of all members; the oath contained the phrase "on the true faith of a Christian," a codicil not removed until 1866. The more pliable Benjamin Disraeli became leader in fact (if not in name) of the Tory party in 1848, but did not become prime minister until 1868 though his party was in power three times in the interim. When Disraeli finally "climbed to the top of the greasy pole" (as he described it), a contemporary called it "a great triumph" of intellect, of courage, of "patience and unscrupulousness employed in the service of a party full of prejudices."

Nor was the England of Gompers's boyhood a happy place for working people, regardless of nationality or religion. The Chartist rebellions of the 1840s, fired largely by worker discontent, had subsided by the time Sam was born, defeated by the depressed economy of the "hungry forties" and by the refusal of British governments to enact meaningful reforms. Few English workers could vote until 1867, and lower-class education scarcely existed until the twentieth century. The few advances made by workingmen resulted from the action of such unions of elite, skilled craftsmen as the Amalgamated Society of Engineers and the Carpenters and Joiners organization. These groups, dominated by native Englishmen such as William Newton and Robert Applegarth, avoided political agitation, cultivated an image of respectability, and focused their efforts on securing gains for their own members rather than on a struggle to ameliorate the conditions of all workers.

Skilled foreign workers like Solomon Gompers emulated their British counterparts, forming conservative craft unions that worked for better wages and working conditions when they could. Most of their energies and resources, however, were devoted to fraternal activities such as providing unemployment, sickness, and death benefits as well as collecting information on job openings. Solomon Gompers believed passionately in his trade union not only because of its economic advantages, but also because it engendered a sense of community and identity among the immigrant cigarmakers, a feeling intensified by their isolation among the British. In the union hall a man could relax, and hear good familiar talk —

about work, about family, about the old country — and he heard it in his native language.

Sam inherited his father's passion for the union. In time it provided the only faith, creed, or religion he needed. In addition, while still a boy, he familiarized himself with the structure and policies of craft unions in England. Throughout the rest of his life he favored organizations patterned after the British model, modified to fit conditions in the New World.

Gompers's situation in London intensified his adherence to the trade-union philosophy. To outsiders, Britain offered little chance of a permanent foothold through social mobility or politics. The Gompers turned inward and drew their sense of identity from the immigrant community, the family, and the workplace. The family — mother, father, and five children — lived in the Spitalfields district of East London in one large room, which functioned as bedroom, sitting room, and kitchen. A small, attached storeroom served as an extra bedroom in the summer. Water had to be fetched from a plug in the street.

The streets were playground and schoolroom. Wandering their narrow, cobbled, smelly lengths, Sam heard the cries of the unemployed and the destitute, begging for work to feed their children. Many were skilled artisans, permanently displaced by machinery. The dislocation provided Sam with a vivid example of the destructive impact of mechanization on a skilled trade.

Young Sam, though small, proved physically powerful. Learning early that "the strong rule in the boy world," he mastered the vicious skills of a street fighter. He used knees, elbows, and deceit to protect himself and his friends. Truculence, bad temper, determination, loyalty, and a willingness to subordinate means to ends served him well in the lanes of London and characterized him all his life, though he learned to temper them with self-control, tact, and Machiavellian skills of manipulation, for he was bright as well as strong.

Sam enjoyed also the rare privilege of more formal schooling. From the ages of six to ten he attended a local free school established by the Jewish community. After leaving school to go to work, he took classes at night. His grandfather, who lived upstairs, broadened Sam's horizons by taking him to plays and concerts, and by telling him stories of countries visited on business. As a result, Gompers at age thirteen, despite his meager formal education, had an acquaintance with the classics in literature, in theater, and in music, a fair fluency in English as well as a rudimentary knowledge of French, Dutch, and Hebrew, a grasp of the folklore of many countries, and a comprehension of European geography. He had also learned basic methods of logical and ethical thought. Altogether he wrought from his "culturally deprived" childhood an armory of intellectual equipment rare among children then or later.

His physical prowess, his encyclopedic memory, and his lifelong eagerness to learn readied him for a successful career in America. The fluid society of the United States more willingly accepted the services of outsiders, whatever their circumstances of birth, than did Britain. Gompers might easily have prospered in business or politics. Indeed, he later declined opportunities to enter both. That he chose to devote his life to the labor movement stemmed largely from the experiences of his youth.

When he was ten, Sam left school to add to the family's income. Briefly apprenticed to a shoemaker, he soon left that trade because of the noise in the shop. His father arranged an apprenticeship to a cigarmaker. After learning the art, he joined his father in the work. Since 1848, Solomon Gompers had belonged to the Cigarmakers' Society, which loosely resembled the British trade unions of the time. The cigarmakers were afflicted with a double liability. Since their product was a luxury item, the trade suffered disproportionately in bad times; moreover, most of the members were immigrants, so their organization had little chance of joining the British trade unions' elite circle.

The union and the atmosphere of the workshop bound the cigarmakers together, providing a feeling of community and a sense of identity. In fact, one of the virtues of Gompers's new trade was the sense, derived from his "father's activity in the Cigarmakers' Society, . . . that there was a society among the cigarmakers but none among the shoemakers." So intensely did Sam absorb the guild mentality that even as a boy of fourteen he felt that he "had been accustomed to the labor movement" all his life, "and accepted as a matter of course that every wage-earner should belong to the union of his trade." This attitude Sam shared with his father, who in later years invariably referred to his son as vice-president of the cigarmakers' union first and as president of the AF of L second. His experiences in the cigarmaking shops of London deepened his sense of pride and community. Cigar-rolling was quiet work, and the men used this advantage by assigning one of their number as reader, sharing their product with him so that he suffered no loss of income. The readers roamed far and wide across the esthetic, political, and economic literature of the time and sampled the current newspapers and magazines. After the readings, the workers engaged in lively, sometimes heated discussions contributing significantly to "the fellowship that grew between congenial shopmates which was something that lasted a lifetime." For Sam, "life in the factory," which proved a Hogarthian nightmare for many, remained "one of [his] most pleasant memories."

The Cigarmakers' Society acted as a mutual aid association, collecting funds to alleviate the members' distress in times of hardship. As part of this policy, the society created an emigration fund for members to go to the United States. The fund offered a double benefit: those who wanted to leave could, and their departure siphoned off excess workers, enhancing the chances of employment for those who remained. In 1863, Solomon Gompers decided to go to America.

The possibilities of immigrant life in America created an irresistible lure to millions, including Solomon Gompers. The

American Civil War, boiling toward a climax when the Gompers family left, heightened the attraction of the United States to many workers in England. Although they suffered as a result of the decline of trade caused by the Union blockade of the Confederacy, British workers regarded the Civil War as a struggle to abolish slavery and to secure permanently the rights of free labor. In the London cigar shop, for example, Sam first heard of Abraham Lincoln, who "symbolized the spirit of humanity." In such a climate, prospective immigrants found poignant meaning in a song:

> To the west, to the west, to the land of the free
> Where mighty Missouri rolls down to the sea;
> Where a man is a man if he's willing to toil,
> And the humblest may gather the fruits of the soil.
> Where children are blessings and he who has most
> Has aid for his fortune and riches to boast.
> Where the young may exult and the aged may rest,
> Away far away, to the land of the west.

In 1848, Andrew Carnegie's father Will had succumbed "To the West" and sailed away from the abandoned hand looms of Scotland. Fifteen years later, Solomon Gompers, with children in plenty and more to come, joined the exodus. Thus there came to the United States from the ends of Great Britain two boys who became America's greatest industrialist and America's foremost labor leader. "To the West" was a siren song indeed.

The Gompers family sailed from England on June 10, 1863, on the *City of London,* which landed them at Castle Garden, New York City, on July 29. During the tedious fifty-day voyage, punctuated by seasickness and a Fourth of July celebration at sea, the crucial events of the American Civil War unfolded. Robert E. Lee suffered the shattering defeat at Gettysburg on July 4 and retreated south for the last time. Ulysses Grant surrounded the Confederate fortress at Vicksburg, Mississippi, starved and fought it into submission (also on July 4), and prepared the campaigns into the Dixie heart-land that ultimately demolished Southern dreams of independence.

The Gompers, however, debarked into a less glorious Civil War battlefield, the streets of New York. The military draft, begun on July 11, had precipitated a series of anticonscription, anti-Negro riots. Mobs of protesters surged through the streets, smashing and looting stores, beating or murdering blacks until forcefully pacified by the Union army on July 16. When the Gompers arrived two weeks later, the city still simmered with midsummer heat and popular indignation. Solomon Gompers discovered inadvertently that tempers could be touched off easily. Shaking hands with a black seaman who had been helpful during the voyage, the father found himself surrounded by angry citizens who threatened to lynch him and the sailor. The incident rudely but appropriately introduced the rough environment of New York in which Sam spent most of the next twenty years.

Fortunately for the Gompers, New York contained friends and relatives as well as hostile strangers. For the Gompers family, as for other immigrants, the move to America was not an impetuous plunge into a totally unknown world but rather a considered act, a conscious decision taken with the aid of money and advice. As one former migrant observed: "The real agents who regulate the . . . movement are the millions of earlier immigrants already in the United States. . . . When the outlook for employment is good, they send for their relatives, or encourage their friends to come."

The Gompers family formed but a single link in one of the long chains that drew thirty-five million Europeans across the Atlantic in the century after 1820. Solomon followed his brother-in-law and numerous friends to America, as he had followed his brother to England. They in turn were followed by at least two dozen cousins, most of them cigarmakers. The family thus landed in a strange country but not entirely among strangers. They were met, as Sam recalled, by relatives and friends, who loaded the family and its possessions on a wagon and carried them to their new home, a four-room apartment in a Houston Street tenement. The neighbors were chiefly Americans, English, and Holland Dutch. Many of the Dutch were cigarmakers, including some whose peregrinations had carried them from the Netherlands to Great Britain and then on to America.

Such familiar neighbors lessened the shock of displacement and allowed Sam to adjust gradually. His occupation contributed to his sense of stability, for he and his father at once went to work rolling cigars at home. The self-sufficient spirit of the immigrant neighborhood, together with his absorption in work, so isolated Sam from the world outside that until the assassination of Lincoln, he felt untouched by the events of the Civil War. Little by little, however, he ventured further into the streets of New York, an education in themselves. Eventually his explorations led him to formative experiences, which augmented the lessons he had learned in the streets and shops of London.

New York in the late nineteenth century was the most ethnically polyglot city in the world. As the principal American entrepôt for European immigrants, it received hundreds of thousands yearly. Most of them passed quickly through the city, moving on to farms or industrial centers. Enough stayed, however, to sustain an immigrant majority among the city's rapidly growing population, which had reached a million by the time the Gompers arrived.

New Yorkers crammed themselves into the lower end of Manhattan Island. In 1863, open country began a mile beyond what is now Times Square. Half the population lived in tenement buildings like the one occupied by the Gompers. Crowding was endemic; it was not unusual to find twelve or fifteen people — family, friends, boarders — occupying two rooms that, in addition to all the normal living functions, doubled as workrooms during the day and early evening. The rooms were small and seldom had windows; the buildings were jammed together. Consequently, the halls and apartments remained submerged in a gloom rarely disturbed by sunlight and dimly lit at night, since good candles and whale-oil lamps were a luxury reserved for festive occasions, and cheap kerosene was not yet available.

Water came from a tap in the backyard, which also held the outhouse, the only sanitary facilities for hundreds of occupants. The yard also served as receptacle for garbage and nastier wastes that cascaded from the windows and lay in heaps of biodegradation. The halls of the tenements matched the squalor of the courtyards, as "the floors and stairs . . . were covered with 'unmentionable filth,' and the walls dripped with slimy exudations." The streets were little better. Teeming with unwashed humanity that threaded its way through the garbage and the horse droppings, the street was marketplace, social center, and playground.

Scattered among the tenements lay a variety of factories. Wholly unregulated by environmental laws or by civic restraint, they pumped their wastes into the streets, air, and water of the town, adding to the miasma that hung over the city, especially on still, humid summer days. Near the Gompers's home were a brewery and a slaughterhouse from which there emanated a stench so unsettling that Sam for a time turned vegetarian. The stink was so potent that one contemporary claimed it poisoned cattle and that no outsider could bear it for more than five minutes.

Somehow in the turbid city sea, Sam found islands of pleasure and excitement. Although he lived in grim surroundings and worked long hours in sweaty lofts, he obviously had a lot of fun. His new locale, noxious though it was, was an improvement over the one left behind in England. More important, his buoyant temperament served him well.

For Gompers, the streets of New York held no terrors after a boyhood spent in the lanes of East London. The four-room tenement apartment, though similar to those which later horrified reformers like Jacob Riis and Jane Addams, gave the family twice as much space as it had squeezed into in London. At thirteen Sam went to work; at fourteen he joined his union; at sixteen he left home and found a job as a journeyman in a local factory; at seventeen he married and found "married life . . . a dream of happiness"; at eighteen he and his wife moved into their own apartment and had their first child. As a journeyman who worked hard and skillfully in a trade in which many idled and malingered, he found steady work at good wages, saved money, and bought "some furniture for which we paid cash — not on time."

Outside the home he found stimulation attending lectures at Cooper Union, an institution established by the industrialist and philanthropist Peter Cooper for "the advancement of sciences and the arts." Off and on for twenty years Sam studied, "fairly quivering" with an intense desire to know, and feeding his "mental hunger which was just as painful as physical hunger" with courses in history, biography, music, mechanics, measurement of speed, elocution, economics, electric power, geography, astronomy, and travels. At Cooper Union he also made many acquaintances, including Peter J. McGuire, an Irish immigrant who later became a trusted lieutenant in the trade-union movement. In addition to enrolling in such courses, Sam found time to continue his London habit of attending plays and concerts and added the popular music hall to his diversions.

Sam also joined several social clubs, including the Order of Foresters and the Odd Fellows. Such organizations attracted him because he met sympathetic companions and because his "idealism and sentiment found expression in fraternalism," which he thought, provided "a chance for men to develop and lend a helping hand when most needed." Although he joined the cigarmakers' local union in 1864, he participated only casually until 1869. He was, he said, "a member of the union . . . for practical reasons." He had yet to learn "that the philosophy and scope of the trade union movement could be made broad and deep enough to include all the aspirations and needs of the wage earner." (Or perhaps he had yet to learn that his own aspirations and needs could be narrowed sufficiently to be encompassed by trade-union service.) In any case, the path that led him to the head of organized labor first opened before him not as a result of his membership in the cigarmakers' union, but because of his decision, taken in 1866, to leave the home workshop and find work as a journeyman, first in the factory of M. Stachelberg, then at other shops in and out of New York.

His skill at work gave him great satisfaction, though not from pride in craftsmanship. Making cigars, though a skilled trade as defined by the times, actually involved as much repetition and as little imagination as the "unskilled" chores of modern assembly lines. Sam liked making cigars, not because they were beautiful (he shared the view expressed by a wag in later times that "a woman is only a woman, but a good cigar is a smoke" — and Sam smoked lots of them), but precisely for the reason now cited for worker dissatisfaction: it did not occupy his mind at all. After a time, he bragged, "a good cigarmaker learned to do [the work] more or less mechanically."

Sam "loved the freedom of that work . . . the mind-freedom . . . which left us free to think, talk, listen, or sing." (A hundred years later the workers at the General Motors plant in Lordstown, Ohio, the most automated, subdivided assembly line in the world, expressed similar sentiments. Few could imagine getting rid of the assembly line, but a good number found ways to make their time at the plant, if not the job itself, more rewarding. "I never think about my job," many of them said, but "doubling" their efforts left half the workers free "to read, lie down, go to the toilet . . . roam the plant and talk to a buddy" or "to sing or whistle.") As always, worker satisfaction depended as much on the atmosphere of the workplace as on the nature of the work.

Like their European counterparts, American cigarmakers maximized the advantages of their trade by employing readers.

Together with the variety of workers who collected in the factories of America, the readings and discussions made Sam's life as a journeyman satisfying and stimulating. In the factory he also observed the haphazard conduct of his trade union. Lacking a systematic philosophy or a practical strategy, the union struggled to maintain wages and improve working conditions by wildcat strikes. The union usually called for work stoppages as a result of an employer's provocation: a pay cut, for instance, or the failure to provide adequate sanitary facilities. It often struck without regard to business conditions and rarely had built up a fund to support its membership during the shut-down. Consequently, the issue was lost as often as won. On occasion Gompers became involved in shop disputes, presenting his colleagues' grievances to his employers. He functioned effectively as both worker and advocate, for Stachelberg once introduced him to a visitor with the comment: "That is Mr. Gompers. . . . He is an agitator, but I don't give a damn, for he makes me good cigars." Such labor activity, however, played little part in Sam's life until the early 1870s. His own casual involvement and the slipshod methods of his union reflected the nature of the industry.

The factories and shops in which Sam worked little resembled those bearing the same titles in later years. They were, in fact, far more typical of the work patterns of the preindustrial world. The factory itself required only a vacant loft equipped with worktables and whatever toilet facilities the proprietor could be badgered into providing. The production process involved no machinery other than the journeymen's hand tools. Since such establishments demanded little capital, workers could, and often did, become bosses overnight.

The workers themselves evinced the casual attitude toward employment characteristic of the more relaxed world of the small farm or the artisan's workshop. They shifted from job to job readily on impulse or the rumor of better conditions.

They worked irregular hours, often of their own choosing, and sometimes no more than a few hours all told. Employers complained that many cigarmakers worked only long enough to provide for their own needs. After two or three hours, they repaired to a nearby saloon (of which there were four thousand in New York) for refreshment. Some days they opted not to work at all. "Saint Monday" was frequently observed, and numerous personal, national, and religious rites justified unscheduled holidays. The employer could retaliate by firing the dilatory, but through the 1860s, when times were good and production unmechanized, an employer antagonized his skilled workers only at peril to his business. He generally found some modus vivendi, some compromise between his interests and his workers' habits. Gompers soon acquired a reputation as a conscientious, skilled worker, which kept him steadily employed at good wages despitè sporadic labor disputes.

In 1869, Gompers at nineteen felt he had made steady progress since coming to America. The New World's promise had turned into a happy reality of family, friends, and work. "Living the absorbing, eager life of a young man," Sam found as much joy in grappling with challenges as in overcoming them. Ever a fighter, he lost none of his truculence as he matured. "At the drop of a hat" he was "ready to fight physically or mentally for any cause to which [he] had given adherence," and he did so often. On one occasion in a saloon frequented by socialists, he mounted a violent defense of American trade unionists. Outraged by criticism of his friends, Sam "jumped up and caught [the offender] by the throat and was shaking the life out of him." Although other tipplers thwarted his homicidal intentions, Gompers recalled with satisfaction, "I forced him into silence." Another time he asked a doctor to attend his wife in childbirth. Learning that Sam had no money, the healer declined to come. Grabbing him by the coat, Sam said: "Yes you will, you will come and see my wife

now . . . or you will never make another move. . . . I will
not be responsible for what I will do to you. Come along." He
came.

At nineteen, Gompers saw himself as an independent man
with much to protect and the ability to protect it. His principal shortcoming, he felt, lay in the need to find an outlet for
his growing talents and for his undiminished energies. By 1869
he had become bored with his lodge brothers, whose company
and conversation no longer interested him. He had grown
conscious of his limitations and of his "inability to express in
words the deep emotions and aspirations that crowded [his]
mind, seeking form and outlet."

The late sixties and early seventies, however, ushered the
harsh realities of the new industrial world into cigar manufacturing, as in so many other American industries. In 1867 a
mold was invented that preformed the cigar filler. Introduced
in 1869, the new machine subdivided the production process
into molding, which untrained workers could perform without
difficulty, and rolling, which still required the traditional
skill. The introduction of the cigar mold provided Sam with
challenges to spare. It also brought to a close the first period of
his life, during which good things had come easily, almost
automatically. Now, in 1869, the lessons he had learned in the
past seemed unavailing in the crisis of the present. Thrusting
himself into the affairs of his union, Gompers began a new
and more rigorous training, one which led to maturity and
leadership.

II

An Old Union Fails
and a New One Is Born
1869–1873

GOMPERS REALIZED at once that the new cigarmaking machinery threatened his comfortable position. At worst it might eliminate his trade altogether; at best it seemed sure to destroy the familiar atmosphere of the shop by flooding it with unskilled workers, many of them Bohemians who spoke neither English nor German (the lingua franca of the cigar trade) and who knew nothing of the traditional pride of the craftsman.

The crisis brought turmoil to the cigarmakers' union. As the organization grappled with the menace of mechanization, Gompers abandoned his other activities and plunged into union affairs. There he found a challenge that lasted the rest of his life. At the outset his efforts exhibited great resolution but an even greater uncertainty. The immediate problem — the cigar mold and the hundreds of unskilled workers (called "bunchbreakers") hired to use it — was met by a strike against the introduction of the machine. The strike failed.

Gompers himself suffered little from the failure, but he learned an invaluable lesson, "the futility of opposing progress." In England and America both, he had witnessed the inevitability of mechanization and the uselessness of resisting it. Some way had to be found to meet the challenge of the machine by keeping the worker in control of it rather than by opposing its introduction.

In 1869 began an economic decline that culminated in the crash of 1873, followed by a general depression lasting until 1879. Employers reacted to the slump by cutting wages and by laying off workers. Strikes against pay cuts generally failed, because rising unemployment made strikebreakers, even skilled strikebreakers, easy to find. Gompers added another lesson to his growing stock of practical principles for trade unions: walkouts had little chance when business declined; prosperity was the time to strike.

A more popular response to the displacements of mechanization was the eight-hour movement, which hoped to ease unemployment by spreading available work. In this agitation Gompers enthusiastically joined. From 1871 to 1874 he attended meetings, listened to speeches, and marched in parades. At such festivities he found himself surrounded not only by his fellow workingmen, but also by a gallimaufry of characters from the gaggle of sects that thrived in cosmopolitan New York. Greenbackers, women's suffragists, prohibitionists, socialists, anarchists — all manner of crackpot philosophers and dedicated reformers made their appearance, each peddling his own particular nostrum as the panacea for society's ills. Some of these indulged in flamboyant, often inflammatory rhetoric. Marchers appeared carrying banners reading: "Peaceably If We Can: Forcibly If We Must," "No More Talk — We Mean Business," "Eight Hours Or Remember."

The growing unrest excited fear and hostility among property owners and public officials, a concern heightened by rumors of communes and "committees of public safety." New York's officials, determined to crush protorevolutionary activities, sent the police to break up an eight-hour rally in Tompkins Square on January 13, 1874. When Gompers arrived at the square, he found "the park . . . packed and all the avenues leading to it crowded." As usual, colorful characters leavened the mass: beautiful Victoria Woodhull, who wore men's clothes and advocated free love; Tom-ri-John, publisher of a paper called the *Emancipator*, printed in red ink and peddled by his wife, who dressed as a man and carried a big stick as a "staff of defense and support," and by their three children, Eruptor, Vesuvia, and Emancipator.

As the rally was about to begin, the mounted police attacked the crowd, indiscriminately clubbing anyone in reach. Gompers escaped by ducking into a cellar. He seethed with indignation at the brutality of the assault, but this and other experiences with the eight-hour movement impressed on his mind two ideas that endured long after his anger had cooled, "fundamentals" that "became guideposts for the labor movement for years to come."

First, he "saw how professions of radicalism and sensationalism concentrated all the forces of organized society against a labor movement and nullified in advance normal necessary activity." Second, he saw that labor must shake off the parasites that clung to it and take control of its own destiny. Many agitators who attached themselves to labor movements *wanted* to antagonize the establishment as a way of pushing society toward some utopian revolution. If radical tactics brought a response that destroyed trade unions, caused business depressions, and provoked police brutality, all of which bore most heavily upon the workers, well, so much the better. Suffering was the necessary cost of doing revolutionary business and hastened the day of retribution and redemption.

Gompers noted that such views most often emanated from people who were not, and often never had been, workers themselves. Then as now there was no shortage of intellectuals and reformers bellowing cant and bawling work songs no worker ever sang. These idealists stood ready to harness labor to the chariot of reform to carry man to the millennium. Such people Gompers determined to expel from labor organizations because he "saw the danger of entangling alliances with intellectuals who did not understand that to experiment with the labor movement was to experiment with human life." Still, Gompers realized that many of the "radical, revolutionary, impatient group were workers and just as sincere as many whose judgment was more dependable."

Among the dependable, two principal types prevailed. First there were the champions of reform through the traditional American political process. Largely American-born, these leaders institutionalized their ideals successively in the National Labor Union and in the Knights of Labor. The second camp consisted of the socialists. Largely European, they distrusted American politics in general and the existing parties in particular. Among the strategies advocated by disparate socialist thinkers, two predominated: direct economic action in the form of strikes and boycotts, and the creation of a labor party built on the trade unions and dedicated to the establishment of a socialist state. Neither method seemed practical to Gompers. Although in time he borrowed from both, in the early seventies he sought other alternatives.

In searching for a new approach, Gompers had to develop a philosophy of action based on hard lessons of experience. He also had to devise an organization to translate principles into effective action. In theory and in practice he had to avoid the folly of ignoring prevailing values. Otherwise he stood no chance to build a movement attractive to workers and congenial to the establishment.

Settling on a philosophy and building an organization took many years. For a union to succeed, the members had to be willing to submit to discipline, which American workers were reluctant to do. Few of them would give up current self-interests to join the march toward some distant goal. As Gompers learned in the early 1870s, labor closed ranks most readily when a new development, such as the cigar mold or a cut in wages, jeopardized its current status. Sometimes workers would rally if unity promised immediate, tangible benefits — like better wages and better working conditions. The eight-hour movement, as Gompers realized, attracted wide support because the shorter workday, if adopted, would protect the employed against the effects of the depression and give them more leisure time, a benefit that grew in attractiveness as laborers became subject to the rigid workday and to the strict discipline of the factory, as opposed to the flexible hours and casual atmosphere of the home, workshop, or farm. Banners at the Tompkins Square rally emphasized labor's view of the relationship between the workday and freedom: "Eight Hours For Work. Eight Hours For Rest. Eight Hours For What We Will."

As a participant in these events, Gompers concluded that no union could expect workers to sacrifice individualism to solidarity unless it found ways to protect or increase their independence. Through the 1870s he sought a workable plan of action. As he himself admitted, "On labor matters my thought was wild," and unsurprisingly so. Although rich in experiences, he was young (twenty in 1870), and he lived in a city where reform theories grew like weeds under the constant fertilization of both native reformers and the European radicals who debarked every immigrant ship. Moreover, he labored in a swiftly changing economic environment. As big firms appeared, they presented American labor with challenges for which no precedent existed.

Fortunately for Gompers, he met early in the decade two men who guided him to an orderly, practical philosophy and who helped him build an organization to implement it. In 1872, he met Adolph Strasser in the Union Hall; in 1873, he met Karl Ferdinand Laurrell at the cigar factory of David Hirsch. Tutored by Strasser and Laurrell and fortified by experience, Gompers emerged in 1881 as vice-president of the Federation of Organized Trades and Labor Unions, the immediate forerunner of the American Federation of Labor. Twelve years after his first groping attempts to find a practical labor strategy, he had become a determined advocate of the method later called "business unionism." He had also developed a vision of the institutional structure needed to put the philosophy in practice — a federation of national unions enrolling workers according to their trade and organized into local, semiautonomous units. In developing his philosophy and building his organization, Gompers sifted through the welter of ideas championed by reformers of varied stripes and hues. Trying this and that scheme, he adopted some and discarded others, an eclectic process based largely on trial and error but often distorted by his personal prejudices. In the end he employed weapons drawn from the arsenal of the two principal schools of thought that dominated American reform movements of the time — the political tactics of the traditional American reformers and the economic methods of the European-oriented socialists. These he fitted to the basic vehicle he had carried in his mind since boyhood, the British trade-union model.

Between the young man of nineteen, casual in his union activities, wild in his labor thought, and inadequately challenged by life, and the seasoned thirty-one-year-old federation officer, following a clear course and absorbed in it night and day, lay twelve years of hard work and bitter experience. In later years, Gompers looked back on those early days as the ground clearing and foundation building of what became a major landmark on the American economic scene. At the time, however, such a destiny was far from manifest.

Unraveling the tangled threads of his life through those twelve years of turmoil, Gompers picked out a series of turning points. His autobiography, *Seventy Years of Life and Labor,* published after his death in 1924, cited these crucial steps in the rise of the trade-union movement to preeminence, respectability, and permanence: (1) the introduction of the molding machine in 1869; (2) the formation of a new local union in 1872–1873, dominated by him, Strasser, and Laurrell, which accepted any cigarmaker who wanted to join, even those who worked with unskilled bunchbreakers, a group then excluded by the existing national union; (3) the recognition of the new local by the old national union in 1875, followed by the election of Gompers as president and of Strasser as financial secretary and by the gradual reshaping of all cigar-makers' locals after the New York model; (4) the strike against a series of wage cuts in 1877, which, though a failure, taught "the fundamentals and technique which assured success later"; (5) the adoption by the national union in 1880 of these fundamentals of business unionism, including high dues, the equalization of funds among locals according to the number of members, and the establishment of sickness, death, and traveling benefits; and (6) the formation in 1881 of the Federation of Organized Trades and Labor Unions, which began coordinating the efforts of individual unions into a systematic strategy.

Organized labor's first halting steps dwindle in significance compared with the giant strides the whole nation took in the same era. The spectacular boom in the country's population, settled areas, and industrial capacity obscured the modest growth of the trade unions. Certainly, few Americans paid much attention to Gompers and his achievements at the time. The heroic figures and cosmic doings that captivated the public's imagination and captured the newspapers' headlines throughout the period relegated labor's vexations to the back pages.

Further, many of labor's specific turning points coincided with some more spectacular incident. In 1869, for example, while Gompers encountered the cigar mold, the transcontinental railroad reached California. This feat stirred visions of a nation stretched "from sea to shining sea, bound together with webs of steel." Between 1869 and 1881, while trade-union membership fell from 300,000 to 200,000, the railroad web expanded from 46,000 to 104,000 miles, opening vast areas of the frontier to settlement. In the same period, while Gompers labored to draw a trickle of adherents to his cause, the waves of immigrants continued unabated. Three-and-a-half million newcomers arrived in those twelve years — fewer than 10 percent of them skilled workers — and fanned out across the country to man its factories and carve the open spaces into farms. Between 1870 and 1880, the number of factory workers rose from 2 million to 2.7 million while output nearly doubled; the number of farms increased from 2.7 million to 4 million, adding to cultivation an area greater than England and France combined.

In 1872–1873, as Gompers, Strasser, and Laurrell created a new local to deal with the recalcitrant cigar shop proprietors of New York, the country reeled under the collapse of Jay Cooke's banking house and staggered into a national depression that lasted six years. In that winter, Andrew Carnegie began construction of the Edgar Thomson Steel Works in Braddock, Pennsylvania. In 1875, when Gompers's new local received its charter, Carnegie began production. The Carnegie works ran day and night, seven days a week, supervised by a bureaucracy of professional managers who labored ceaselessly to increase production and cut expenses by substituting machinery for manpower and by slashing the wages of the workers who remained. While Gompers roamed the streets of New York, busying himself with the problems of a trade with patterns of ownership and methods of production rooted in the past, the future loomed 400 miles away on the banks of the Monongahela River in the bleak walls and smokestacks of the Carnegie works.

Gompers struggled to shape craft workers into a disciplined force that could exert bargaining leverage at the same time that Carnegie and his imitators whittled steadily away at the employers' dependence on skilled labor. As industrialists poured capital into machinery housed in massive factories, the output of handicraft shops fell from 50 percent of manufactured goods in 1870 to 20 percent in 1890. Inside the factories mechanical devices and assembly lines gradually eliminated skilled tradesmen from production, though they remained important in design and maintenance.

In 1877, Gompers and his associates led the unsuccessful

strike in which they learned "the fundamentals and technique" for the future. Other events, however, claimed the country's attention. In the West, the army recovered from Custer's debacle of the year before, routed Sitting Bull and his Sioux warriors in the Dakotas, and crushed the Nez Perce rebellion in Oregon. In the South, Reconstruction ended when the last federal troops departed from South Carolina and Louisiana, as Rutherford B. Hayes fulfilled the bargain with Southern conservatives that broke the deadlocked presidential election of 1876 and ended the most serious constitutional crisis since secession. In the Northeast, railroad workers, stung by a series of pay cuts, exploded in a spreading paroxysm of violence, burning locomotives, cars, and buildings, tearing up track, and occupying property. This eruption thoroughly frightened the financial and political establishment. Police, militia, vigilantes, and federal troops assaulted the strikers up and down the line, restoring order through superior violence.

Besides being obscured by more tempestuous events, Gompers's achievements attracted little attention because they involved relatively few people. In addition, they generated little sympathy not only because they seemed to be part of the general worker unrest threatening the national stability, but also because Gompers and his followers constitued a privileged elite in American society. The movement that grew into the AF of L, 1.7 million strong in 1904, began with a small band of cigarmakers. All trade unionists together totaled only 4.9 percent of the nonfarm labor force in 1870; by 1880 even this small foothold had loosened to 2.3 percent.

The skilled tradesmen who enrolled in these organizations already enjoyed a more fortunate social and economic status than most of their fellow citizens. Indeed, the threat in the 1870s to the prestige and prosperity to which craftsmen were accustomed did far more to stimulate union activity than did any promises for future improvement. The movement began as a holding action by a threatened elite. It drew little sympathy from people who felt worse off. Black freedmen in the South, native American Indians and Chinese coolies in the West, farmers on the prairie, unskilled immigrants in the cities, laborers in the factories, women in sod huts and tenements, felt slight kinship to Gompers and his ilk with their little bank accounts and their big airs, their time to spare for philosophical discussions in saloons and meeting halls, and their natty silk hats and Prince Albert coats. The climb to power, prestige, and permanence proved hard for trade unionists; often they suffered privations, beatings, and imprisonment. Nevertheless, they made swift progress up the ladder, because they traveled light, took few with them, and started nowhere near the bottom.

At the beginning of his serious involvement in trade-union affairs, Gompers observed the events of 1869–1872 and assembled a catalog of negative experiences. Strikes against the introduction of machinery failed. So did strikes against wage cuts and strikes for an eight-hour day. He could see the futility of precipitate, uncoordinated work stoppages, particularly when business was bad and when unions had accumulated no funds to support the strikers. Violence and radical rhetoric aroused opposition and set back the cause. Learning what tactics had not worked in the past did not teach him what methods might avail in the future. While pondering the lessons of failure, Sam shopped around for ideas that might lead to success.

In New York's seething intellectual marketplace, the prevailing commodity was socialism, offered in a variety of brands. The two most popular were Lassallean and Marxist. The former, the doctrine of the German theorist Ferdinand Lassalle, advocated reform through politics and to a degree resembled the traditional American approach. The Lassalleans wanted to build a socialist political party, beginning with a core of urban labor and expanding to absorb enough of the poor and propertyless to collect an electoral majority. Once the workers controlled the state, it would advance the capital to set up factories run as workers' cooperatives. Such third parties were not new to American politics. The Republican party itself had begun as one. Even workingmen's parties had appeared at times in local and national political contests, but they soon capsized from internal dissension, lack of popular appeal, or both.

Past failures did not deter the American Lassalleans. They wanted a socialist party, and they established one. In fact, they established several as time passed and doctrinal differences flared. The young Gompers, however, found little appeal in this approach. The problems were immediate; the mills of politics ground slowly. He himself could not vote until 1871, in any case, and even when he could, he realized that his and all workingmen's votes together could never constitute a majority. The Lassallean answer to this dilemma was to seek allies, but Sam had already concluded, in Tompkins Square and elsewhere, that labor's putative allies too often were its undoing.

The other brand of socialism, Marxist, proved more attractive. Although it too favored long-run reform through political action, it also demanded immediate improvement of the workers' lot, advocated direct economic action such as strikes and boycotts to enforce the demands, and thought that trade unions, not political parties, were the right weapon to cannonade the walls of the capitalists' fortress. Furthermore, Marxist socialism provided stalwarts with a compelling rhetoric to rally labor's troops. In a country where long-prevailing doctrine legitimized the ownership and defense of private property and thus made the capitalist business system right, only a powerful counterargument could persuade many that the system was wrong, thereby justifying the abolition or redistribution of private wealth.

Marxism provided such a justification in the labor theory of value. This doctrine argued that the value of all products came from the labor that went into them. Labor was therefore entitled to all the benefits. This clearly was one of the natural laws, extrapolated from nature's eternal verities, which seemed likely to replace the obsolete irrationalities of religion and philosophy. When natural laws conflicted with man-made laws, the discrepancy demanded stringent remedial measures. In late nineteenth-century America, precedents existed for rebellions justified by natural law, not the least of them the American Revolution. The Declaration of Independence had declared it necessary "to dissolve the political bands" that had connected the colonies to Great Britain, so as "to assume among the Powers of the earth, the separate and equal station to which the Laws of Nature and of Nature's God entitle them."

The same doctrine of natural law served capital as well as labor, for it lent itself readily to the defense of vast accumulations of wealth by individuals. Darwinism, transferred by Herbert Spencer from the realm of the giraffe and the orangutan into the human arena and packaged for popular consumption into the catch phrase "survival of the fittest," eased many a millionaire's conscience. Among those soothed was Carnegie. When he read Spencer, Carnegie said, "Light came in as a flood and all was clear. . . . I got rid of the theology and the supernatural [and] found the truth of evolution. 'All is well since all grows better' became my motto, my true source of comfort."

Marx's doctrine of the labor theory of value made it possible to argue persuasively for the destruction of capitalism by claiming that it siphoned off much of the value created by labor. The correction of this and of other distortions of capitalism would inevitably come through the proletarian revolution when the workers would cast off their chains, then establish a dictatorship of the proletariat that would later metamorphose into a stateless communist nirvana.

By the 1870s, sympathizers on both sides of the Atlantic had concluded that revolutions might be a long time a-coming and might do more harm than good when the great day arrived. Consequently, they decided to nudge the process forward and update it a bit along the way. After all, if the same general end could be achieved without blood running in the scuppers or without throwing all private property down to the candlesticks into the common pot, why not? The problem was finding the right substitute for violent revolution. Thus the split among the American socialists in Gompers's time.

The Marxist wing attracted Gompers because it emphasized immediate results, economic action, and trade unions. The rhetoric appealed to him as well, though he knew it must be used with care so as not to alarm the public. It provided a philosophical counterweight to capitalism, one equally vindicated by natural law, and it offered an alternative plan of action to the other legitimate method of reform, democratic politics. To Gompers and many of his European cohorts, politics was usually sluggish and often treacherous. Most socialists had come from autocratic countries like Germany, or from England, where democracy was a privilege restricted to a few and served to maintain, not level, class distinctions. What they observed in the United States, where the Tammany Hall politics of New York mirrored the corruption of Grant's national administration, did little to alleviate their cynicism.

The socialists' lingo appealed to Gompers's emotions as well as to his logic. Although his easy, gregarious work in the cigar shops scarcely qualified him as one of the "downtrodden, toiling masses," and although his bosses, usually only a few years removed from the workbench themselves, were small fry compared with such genuine capitalist exploiters as Carnegie, the Vanderbilts, and Jay Gould, the socialists' belligerence stirred his naturally combative spirit. It also, he thought, furnished the kind of propaganda that might rally workers to the trade-union banner.

How much of this bombast Gompers believed, and when, is hard to know. He certainly mastered the socialist language and used it often. Beyond some point in his career, he probably employed it more as a tool of internal union politics than as an expression of his own convictions. In the early 1870s, however, it doubtless provided a forceful expression of his frustrations with the evolving menace of industrial capitalism.

Socialism also piqued his intellectual curiosity. He learned German to pursue the original writings of Marx, Lassalle, and others. But socialism in America proved not the highroad to paradise but a blind alley to nowhere, as socialist leaders burned up their energies in doctrinal disputes, splintering the faithful into bickering tribes instead of massing them into a disciplined army. Socialism, as one historian described it, was "a flood of short-lived organizations, quickly rising and even more quickly falling; a vast quadrille [of] political and economic groups, often moving in opposite directions, constantly changing partners, occasionally all joining together for one brief turn only to separate again immediately to form some new pattern."

Endless accusations and counteraccusations of apostasy and blasphemy drew support from speeches and tracts showing why this was the one true faith and that was not. Often the chieftains seemed more concerned with arguing whether socialist angels could dance on the head of Adam Smith's capitalist pin than with finding ways to take over the pin factory. The American socialists also suffered another liability common to revolutionaries: the need to show their colleagues that they genuinely rejected the prevailing establishment. Orthodoxy became desperately important. Doctrinal deviation suggested subversion by the enemy. Capitalism had proved a surprisingly seductive subverter, especially in England, where radical politicians and trade-union leaders with alarming regularity abandoned the cause of the commonality for the manors and manners of the gentry. Consequently, socialists and union leaders in America as elsewhere often spent as much time defending themselves against attacks from the rear as they did assaulting the enemy front.

Gompers himself enjoyed no immunity. Even in the 1870s, when he frequently proclaimed himself a socialist and flung class epithets with the best of them, he faced accusations of apostasy and deviationism. In later decades, as he pursued his policy of accommodating the labor movement to the realities of capitalism, he repeatedly defended himself against the charge of class collaboration and hotly denied ever abandoning the workers' cause. Gompers, however, never thought socialist metaphysics a substitute for practical trade-union activity, nor talk a substitute for action. He never succumbed to the paralysis of logic chopping. His common sense checked his imagination whenever it strayed too far from practicality and enabled him to see that the Marxists, despite their advocacy of immediate economic action and workers' organizations, had little to suggest in the way of remedies for the trade unions' shortcomings. In fact, the lack of organizational ability among the leadership plagued American socialism as much as did internal dissension. Shopping for practical ways to shore up the unions' flimsy structure, Gompers found little he could buy at the socialist rummage sale, so he searched elsewhere.

In 1870 Gompers went to Cooper Union to hear an Englishman, A. J. Mundella, "speak on the scope and influence of trade unions." Mundella, a Nottingham manufacturer, "established the first voluntary board of conciliation and arbitration" for disputes in the glove and hosiery trades. Gompers attended because he was "interested to know what changes had come among British workers after [he had] left England as a lad of thirteen." What he heard disappointed him, for he could see no way, given the independent attitude of workers and employers, for American labor to try cooperation or arbitration, the remedies Mundella suggested. At this gathering, as at so many labor meetings of the seventies, he "found passionate feeling, idealism, but little practical aid." The inapplicability of recent British developments to the American context reconfirmed his faith in the English "new model unions" he had observed in his boyhood.

Adolph Strasser and Ferdinand Laurrell, who entered his life in 1872-1873, also helped Gompers steer clear of the socialist morass. Strasser, whom Gompers met at a union meet-

ing, remained something of a mysterious figure, declining to
discuss his past. "No one ever questioned another as to his past
life, for many were revolutionists who sought new opportunity
and safety by leaving the past blank." All Gompers ever
learned for certain was that Strasser was Hungarian by birth,
seemed to have some money of his own, and apparently
learned cigarmaking late in his life.

Strasser sought new opportunity on a course that paralleled
and then converged with Gompers's own. First he delved into
socialism, though he favored the Lassallean variety. For a time
he served as president of the Social Democratic party. Gradually he abandoned socialist activism because, according to
Gompers, "the old dispute between the dogmatic Lassalleans
and the Marxian trade unionists prevented the Social Democratic Party either from unifying the labor groups or from
developing an agency that would serve the . . . American
workingmen." Strasser also wearied of the socialists' endless
debates over philosophy — "sophistry," he called it — and he
"shifted all his energy to the trade union movement." Strasser's
energy, coupled to his iron will and harnessed by self-
discipline and a passion for organization, made him a powerful ally, a persuasive guide, and a dominant figure in the
union. Gompers called him the "Bismarck of the cigarmakers."

Gompers met his other mentor, Ferdinand Laurrell, in the
cigar factory of David Hirsch, where Sam went to work in
1873. Hirsch was a curious sort of capitalist, for he had
been expelled from Germany for socialist activities, had
moved to New York, and had gone into business, thus demonstrating the relative ease with which one could move from
worker to employer. Hirsch's shop attracted many of his fellow
socialists, one of whom was Laurrell. Born in Sweden, Laurrell
spent two years at sea before coming ashore to learn cigarmaking in Copenhagen. He joined the International Workingmen's Association — the "First International," the Marxist
labor movement sanctioned by Marx himself — and became
secretary of the Scandinavian section. Expelled from Copen-

hagen for demonstrating outside the royal palace, he moved to Hamburg and thence to New York.

Laurrell was a hard-bitten character, disenchanted equally by politics and by airy socialist theories. He told Gompers that his son was destined to become governor of New Jersey. "He has all the qualifications," Laurrell said. "He cusses, he cheats, and he lies." Gompers met Laurrell at a time when Sam's intoxication with the heady brew imbibed at socialist meetings was at its peak. He brought his ideas to Laurrell, who refuted them logically, point by point. After one such encounter, Sam vowed: "Never again will I talk that stuff — but I will find principles that will stand the test."

Laurrell, however, did not confine his educational efforts to tearing away young Gompers's illusions. "Groping for something fundamental," Gompers recalled, "something upon which one could base a constructive program," he spoke to Laurrell of his need. "If you wish to know," Laurrell replied, "I will give you something tangible, something that will give you a background philosophy." The something was a copy of Marx's *Communist Manifesto* in German (a language Gompers had not yet learned), which Laurrell translated and elaborated, paragraph by paragraph. Here, Laurrell argued, lay the key to the workers' plight, but it could not be grasped through dedication to hopeless causes or to irrelevant ideas, such as those promulgated by socialists. "Go to their meetings," he advised Gompers, "listen to [them] and understand them, but do not join the Party." "I know it sounds churlish and unjust to destroy one's god," Laurrell said, "fools though they may be. It is never a gracious task to perform the duty of an iconoclast, but one of these days you will thank me for it." (He was right; Gompers dedicated his autobiography to "Ferdinand Laurrell . . . who was my mental guide through many of my early struggles.")

Laurrell also provided Gompers with a crucial bit of advice that helped him shift from zealotry to eclecticism. Whenever Gompers proposed some new notion, Laurrell would say,

"Study your union card Sam, and if the idea doesn't square with that, it ain't true." This guiding principle freed Gompers from the straitjacket of philosophical orthodoxy. The overriding test of any theory became its effect on the trade-union movement. If the idea advanced the union's cause by adding membership or by helping win a confrontation with employers, then it should be adopted; if not, it should be discarded — in either case without reference to the idea's place in some philosophical catechism. Gompers's adherence to this maxim explains how he borrowed freely over the years from conflicting dogmas and combined them into a cohesive strategy. It also moved him into the American mainstream, for pragmatic policies based on trial and error always dictated action in the United States.

Gompers's ability to weld a coalition of conflicting ideas and their followers also served him well in the American environment, where no political party ever survived lacking a philosophy flexible enough to attract hostile groups without demanding that they reconcile their differences. To insist that Americans abandon their individualism in the name of organizational unity based on an ideology was to court failure. Gompers managed to enlist support among white, male, skilled workers across a spectrum of trades, national origins, and religions, many of them antagonistic. His failure to extend the movement to minority groups, women, and the unskilled resulted, among other reasons, from his inability to broaden his philosophy enough to draw new followers without alienating the old ones.

In 1872 and 1873, however, when Gompers and Strasser began to organize a new union, they started with a nucleus of homogeneous elements, a handful of cigarmakers in New York. They had yet to formulate a comprehensive program, but they had relegated idealistic theories to a distant second place behind immediate, practical actions, carried out by the workers themselves. Early in his career as a labor leader, then, Sam exhibited the pragmatism and the eclecticism that remained his hallmarks thereafter.

III

The New Union Matures and a Federation Emerges
1873–1881

IN 1872, only three years after his first serious involvement in union affairs, Gompers had matured enough to become Strasser's chief lieutenant in the cigarmakers' union. Together they masterminded a counterattack against the forces that threatened to eliminate skilled workers from the cigar trade. Meeting the crisis in New York necessitated a new local union and new principles of trade-union operation. These methods — business unionism — were then introduced into the cigarmakers' national organization. Business unionism worked so well that Gompers saw it as the universal remedy for all labor's ills and considered himself just the man to administer the medicine. By 1881 he had risen from obscurity to national prominence, and he aspired to leadership of the American labor movement.

The introduction of the cigar mold permitted manufacturers to shift from factories and shops to the tenements. They bought or rented blocks of flats and sublet them to cigar workers — many of them Bohemians. The workers bought their materials from the manufacturer, carried them home, rolled the cigars, and resold them to the manufacturer. The workers existed in a state of semibondage, receiving very little in cash after deductions for rent and materials. The balance was often paid in cigars or in credit at the company store, conveniently located on the tenement's ground floor. Survival in these conditions often required that the whole family — men, women, and children — work long hours every day.

The tenement method put the old practitioners in a desperate fix. By 1872 Gompers's own local, which once had hundreds of members, had fewer than fifty left. Furthermore, the national union (the Cigarmakers' International) refused to change its regulations to meet new conditions in New York and let unskilled workers join. The "westerners" in Detroit and Chicago dominated the union. Since they did not confront the tenement system in their cities, they could not appreciate the difficulties of their fellows in the East. Largely American-born and steeped in the guild mentality, they refused to sanction organization of the unskilled, whether in shops or tenements, and forbade their members to work in the same shops with bunchbreakers.

Faced with such intransigence, many New York cigarmakers saw no choice but to drop out. Strasser, however, had another plan and he enlisted Gompers's support. Retaining their membership in the old local, they simultaneously created a new union, the United Cigarmakers, which drew its membership from the old English- and German-speaking locals of the Cigarmakers' International Union. In addition, they threw open the doors to both factory and tenement workers, regardless of degree of skill. By creating a new union in a trade where an old one already existed, Gompers and his colleagues committed one of the trade unionists' cardinal sins, dual unionism. They felt justified because it seemed a matter of life or death (an excuse Gompers fell back on often to defend similar acts in later years) and because they retained their membership in the old union. In addition, they immediately opened a campaign to get the national union to approve their actions and to revise its rules according to the Manhattan model.

In the years that followed, this process created the American

Federation of Labor. The New York cigarmakers developed a plan of attack and an organization to press it home; the national union gradually adopted them; other crafts followed. Gompers and Strasser thus turned the strategy of the socialists and their intellectual allies upside down. Instead of assembling an elite crew of leaders, creating an organization, assigning it a high-flown name, and then setting out with a theoretical program to recruit a rank and file, Gompers and Strasser worked from the bottom up. Full-time workers themselves, they wanted no other kinds of members. If a cigarmaker happened to be a socialist — or a Republican, a Democrat, or a Greenbacker for that matter — that was his business. On the other hand, no nonworker could qualify simply by membership in a political group, however sympathetic it might be to labor's cause. Gompers adopted this position at the outset, supported by Stasser and Laurrell, and he never retreated from it.

Instead of agitating for reform of the national political or economic system, the United Cigarmakers focused on improving conditions in their own trade and locale. Not someday. Now. Even though Gompers at the start may well have favored abolition of capitalism and the creation of a workers' state of some kind, he had no intention of waiting for that happy day for improvement of his situation. For the moment, he concentrated on enrolling members and launching an assault for higher pay and better working conditions. In time the means came to be the end, and he concluded that American workers could achieve all their goals — social, political, and economic — by getting more money in fewer hours under better conditions.

The campaign for new members progressed slowly, as did the drive to reform the national cigar union. By 1875, Gompers's efforts, hampered by the depression, had raised the membership to 245, modest enough, but the largest cigar local in the United States. In 1872 the national rescinded the restriction against members working in the same shop as bunchbreakers. In 1875 it agreed to admit all workers "regardless of sex, method or place of work, or nationality." Gompers's group then applied for and received a charter from the national, becoming Local 144 of the Cigarmakers' International, with Gompers as president and Strasser as financial secretary.

Local 144's constitution employed a language drawn from socialist rhetoric:

We recognize the solidarity of the whole working class to work harmoniously against their common enemy — the capitalists. . . . United we are a power to be respected; divided we are the slaves of the capitalists.

Theoretical solidarity, however, did little to induce unity. Native workers never believed in the idea of a working class anyway, while the immigrants came with the idea of raising themselves, or at least their children, out of it rather than locking themselves and their posterity into it.

Gompers and Strasser designed a program to produce immediate results. The first priority was getting control of organized labor's fundamental weapon, the strike. To this end Local 144 set up a mechanism to prevent indiscriminate walkouts. Each shop with seven or more members constituted a discrete unit that met weekly. Workers from other shops were organized into district units ("locals") of two hundred or less. Strike proposals first had to be approved by a secret ballot within shop organizations, then passed to the local's board of administration. If the board approved, it supplied financial aid and appointed a committee to direct the confrontation.

The local concentrated its attacks on shops with the lowest-paid workers. Such shops found it most difficult to attract strikebreakers. Furthermore, although Gompers often declared that "the capitalists are united," he knew that employers as often behaved like sharks as like sheep. Since low-wage bosses provided the stiffest competition, their better-paying colleagues had little incentive to come to the aid of the miserly.

Should the board of administration decide against a proposed walkout, the members were expected to acquiesce. Gompers urged his followers to "behave like a well-drilled and disciplined army." "It is not wise or practical," he added, "to *at all times strike, even against a reduction of wages. . . .* If a reduction . . . cannot be successfully resisted, accept; but maintain your organization, for by that means . . . only can we . . . regain our lost ground, and even something more." Although mutinies sometimes occurred, the disaffected had little chance without financial support from the local. Worse yet, Gompers and Strasser ruthlessly enforced discipline by supplying the employer with loyal unionists to break wildcat strikes. Finally, the plan gained support because it worked. Choosing opportune targets and propitious moments, the cigarmakers' percentage of success rose steadily, particularly after the return of prosperity in 1879–1880. Between 1881 and 1883, for example, the Cigarmakers' International received 218 applications for strikes, approved 194, and won about 75 percent of them.

Gompers became official organizer for the Cigarmakers' International in 1875, a role he had filled for his local since its formation in 1872. It was a tough job. He trudged the streets of New York to talk to workers in shops and tenements. He learned the art of speechmaking, overcoming a tendency to stammer. He wrote pamphlets in English and German and had them translated into Bohemian. He sent circular letters to cigarmakers all over the country, urging the merits of the New York plan and exhorting them to join the cause. He did all this while working a ten-hour day, receiving no pay for his union work; he derived enormous energy from dedication. He gloried in the struggle and cherished each little victory. "We fought for each gain and with bare hands unaided carried off victories against the protest of a hostile world." Strengthened by his conviction that "life was an adventure, not a tragedy," he regarded defeats as temporary.

To provide an incentive to new members and to sustain them once in the fold, Gompers and Strasser installed a program of financial benefits lifted almost intact from British trade unions' policies. Gradually the New York local established a system of payments for strikers as well as sick pay and death benefits. The union lent money to members who had to travel from one area to another to find work.

The funds for all this came from high dues, a policy on which Gompers always insisted. He hated "Cheap John Unionism"; it led to organizations that could not resist employers or attract members. "There is not a dollar which the working man or woman pays into a labor organization which does not come back a hundredfold," he declared. Low wages were no excuse; let the union become weak, and employers would cut them further, and the "money you refused to pay into your union as dues will go into the coffers of the employers." Furthermore, high dues would attract, not repel, prospective members, because they would see that modest premiums bought comprehensive insurance. Finally, Gompers argued, the richer a union was, the less it was likely to have to spend its money. Employers who confidently rejected demands from a few workers relying on nothing but their own resources would think twice when confronted by a shop group backed by a strong organization with a big strike fund at its disposal.

One by one the New York local introduced these concepts of business unionism and secured their adoption by the national union, which added a provision for equalization of funds among locals. This plan, which Gompers copied from the British engineers' union, in effect pooled the financial resources of all locals, enabling them to draw on the combined assets in times of need, just as shop organizations had access to the treasury of the entire local. It took until 1881 to win acceptance of the whole business union plan, but it soon paid dividends. Between January and September, 1881, Local 144's membership rose from less than three hundred to more than three thousand.

Gompers and Strasser used their political skills to transplant the New York program into the national body. In 1875,

Strasser became vice-president of the Cigarmakers' International. As Gompers recalled, "We planned to utilize that connection for getting the principles we had evolved carried over into the trade organization." At the national convention in 1877 Gompers pulled off a coup d'etat that made Strasser president. After several deadlocked ballots failed to elect a chief, Gompers suggested that the delegates fill other offices first and then disposed of Strasser's rivals by getting them elected to vice-presidencies. According to Gompers, Strasser's

administration began a new era for the Cigarmakers and for all trade unions . . . the beginning of a period of growth, financial success and sound development . . . a period during which uniform regulations, high dues, union benefits, union label, better wages, and the shorter work-day were established.

Strasser's achievements were largely restricted to building an organization. The structure he built rested on a political underpinning characteristically American, for he had the difficult task of welding into one organization "the representative sons of many nations." Unfortunately, he lacked one trait essential to politicians: "He did not have that quality of conciliation necessary to bring the struggle to a satisfactory conclusion." Gompers supplied the needed gift for compromise, which he had in plenty; too much so, his critics often claimed, then and since. Such criticisms overlooked a basic fact of life in American trade unions. They behaved internally like political parties. The membership included heterogeneous elements and tended to be highly issue-oriented, inert unless provoked by a specific grievance. Thus, most of the work fell on a handful of the dedicated or opportunistic.

Elected labor leaders, like politicians, often faced the choice of pleasing a majority of their constituents so as to get re-elected or of following their consciences to defeat. Labor leaders therefore tried to build machines through patronage to deliver the vote; they hedged on difficult questions; and they told each group of constituents what it wanted to hear, even if that meant contradicting a previous declaration. Gompers used all these tactics. Gompers, one critic declared, "could sound very radical indeed . . . when writing to an International Socialist Congress. . . . Addressing . . . business leaders he could sound very conservative." When the workers gave off radical vibrations, "Gompers could voice radical sentiments." When times changed, "he could easily repudiate each and every one of his earlier progressive utterances" and become "the leading opponent of what he had previously championed."

He could scarcely have done anything else and maintained his hegemony. He made decisions based on his estimate of "what would advance the interests of Samuel Gompers and further his career as president of the AF of L" and supported "a progressive program as long as it would advance his career," and no longer. Such was the nature of American politics.

For better or worse, Americans exhibited no tendency to abandon their society's dominant attitudes toward individualism, mobility, property, and democracy when dealing with problems associated with their jobs. Quite the contrary. To succeed, a labor organization had to develop a program in harmony with these prevailing beliefs.

Gompers sensed this from the beginning. "We promot[ed] our local with a feeling of high consecration to principles of human freedom and democracy," American-style. By making sure each member had a copy of the organization's constitution, and by making strikes and officials a matter of ballot, "the union grew slowly and steadily [as] a genuinely American trade union." Since voting determined policy, Gompers and his colleagues felt the franchise had to be restricted to those immediately concerned — the workers — because they had to make the sacrifices necessary to build the organization and carry out its strategies. This justified the exclusion of outsiders. "The labor movement must consist of trade unionists and be controlled by them," Gompers argued, claiming that such a policy was supported by "the democratic theory that wage earners understood their problems and could deal with them better than outsiders." Adhering to these policies, justified in the sacred name of democracy, "developed the principles upon which the first real American trade union was . . . grounded."

The earliest serious test of the "real American trade union" came in 1877. Despite Gompers's efforts, the union had made only slow progress until then, hampered by the continuing depression and set back by an unsuccessful strike against a wage cut in 1876. In June, 1877, the violent railroad strike broke out. "Heartened by the courage of the railway workers' protest," the cigarmakers decided to make a stand and struck the De Barry shop, demanding higher wages. After five weeks the strike succeeded, as did several others.

This victorious campaign, Local 144's first, had two immediate consequences. One, dozens of cigarmakers hurried to climb aboard the bandwagon. The union's secretary, Louis Berliner, found himself besieged by applicants, one of whom demanded more speed: "I have been waiting here fifteen minutes." "You are a nice duck to talk to me about fifteen minutes," Berliner retorted. "I have been waiting here for you for fifteen years."

The other fruit of victory proved more difficult to accept. Seeing the success of the trade unionists, the tenement cigar workers struck en masse. The local chieftains at first had little sympathy because the "tenement house scum" (as Strasser called them) had contributed nothing to building up the union, and their willingness to work for starvation wages had hampered the organization at every turn. Moreover, the tenement workers had no money, no organization, and no discipline. The local's membership, less pragmatic and vindictive than its leaders, voted to back the new walkout. The strikers' descriptions of their dismal working and living conditions and the union's desire to organize the whole trade prevailed over practical considerations.

The local tried to persuade the better paid among the

strikers to go back to work in order to support the others, but to no avail; once released, the hostilities could not be corked up again. Then the National Cigar Manufacturers' Association declared a lockout, cutting off the union's principal source of income. On the brink of losing everything so recently gained, the union decided to fight it out and declared a general strike. The manufacturers retaliated by evicting striking workers from the tenements, throwing whole families into the street in the dead of winter.

The union fought on as best it could. Handicapped by having only $4,000 in the treasury, they appealed for money to members all over the country. They bought a building and set up their own factory, with Gompers as superintendent. They rented rooms for evicted strikers, set up soup kitchens, and distributed food. At the height of the strike eleven thousand workers participated. In all, the union spent $40,000, an unprecedented sum — but not enough. Gradually the strike petered out as the workers gave up the struggle and returned to their jobs. The manufacturers' association blacklisted the leaders.

For a time Gompers found no work, and his family, by now grown to six children, fell into desperate straits. Gompers pawned everything of value except his wife's wedding ring. Sometimes the family had nothing to eat but a soup of flour, water, salt, and pepper. Finally, Laurrell came to the rescue with a job at Matthew Hutchinson's factory. Hutchinson, an independent sort, heard his workers say that the employers had combined to blacklist Gompers. "Who in hell says the bosses have combined?" Hutchinson demanded. "I haven't combined and I will employ who I please and to hell with the others. . . . Tell Gompers to come here and I will give him a job."

Although the strike had not succeeded, Gompers regarded it as a turning point in the trade-union movement. The organization had stood up well under a difficult and unexpected test. It had marshaled and coordinated an army of workers, feeding

and housing many of them. The long strike had hurt the
employers badly, too; they had lost considerable income, and
the economic pressure had caused dissension in their ranks.
Thereafter they proved more tractable.

Gompers no doubt looked back on 1877 as a crucial time for
personal as well as organizational reasons. After the strike, he
concluded that he must withdraw from the local's affairs
(though not of course from membership) to rebuild his
family's dilapidated fortunes. He moved to the Williamsburg
section of Brooklyn and managed to pass up meetings for one
miserable week. The second week he stayed in Manhattan for
the meeting, had to eat at a restaurant, and did not get home
until two o'clock in the morning. Successive meetings continued to drain his finances and energies. "I saw the situation
was hopeless . . . and concluded it was no use; we moved
back to [Manhattan], and if possible, with more zest and
energy [I] re-entered the struggle. . . . That, in my opinion,
was the turning point in my life."

Certainly it marked the last time personal considerations
overrode service to the union. For Gompers, the union was his
life. It provided him with occupation, avocation, entertain-
ment, support for his ego, and an outlet for his powerful
ambitions. After a day spent at work, followed by an evening
at a meeting, he usually finished up in a saloon with his
cronies. He sought no friends outside those he made in the
line of work and duty, though he later enjoyed becoming the
familiar of the presidents and industrialists he met in his
union role. He declined all offers to leave the ranks of the
workers or the offices of the trade union, passing up opportunities to become a law clerk, a foreman, a manufacturer. He
refused to run for office, and turned down Senator John Sherman's offer of a $2,000-a-year sinecure as a statistician in the
Treasury Department, even though the job would have
doubled his salary and left him free to devote full time to
labor organizing. In 1880 he was reelected president of Local
144, and for the rest of his life held office in either the local or

national union of his trade, or in the AF of L. He never retired. When he died, he was the federation's president and had been president every year but one since its founding in 1886.

In all of this he enjoyed his wife Sophie's unstinting support. Although they married almost on a whim to celebrate Sam's seventeenth birthday (she was sixteen) at the end of a brief and casual courtship, the marriage stood every strain put on it. The couple had ten or twelve children. (Gompers could never remember which, a comment on his own priorities as well as on the mortality rates of the times. Only four of the children lived to be forty.) Bearing them, raising them, often watching them die, Sophie showed mettle and a commitment to Sam's cause as great as his own. During the aftermath of the great strike of 1877, while the family subsisted on flour soup, one of Sophie's former suitors called and offered her thirty dollars a week (about twice Sam's normal salary) for three months if she would persuade Sam to give up the union. "What did you tell him?" Sam asked when he heard the story. "What do you suppose I said to him with one child dying and another coming? Of course I took the money." Gompers relates that he was so "stunned by the blow" that he "fell in a chair," recovering only when Sophie added, "Good God, Sam, how could you ask such a question? Don't you know I resented the insult?"

When Gompers returned to the union wars, then, he did so sure in the knowledge of unquestioning support at home. He exhibited enormous zest and energy in the campaigns that followed the 1877 strike. The first of these was an assault on the tenement-house manufacturing system. In 1878 Local 144 held a mass protest meeting at which Gompers made the principal speech. He called the tenements "dens of filth and disease, prisons for small children, and a source of gross immorality and crime." The meeting called on Congress to abolish tenement production and on the commissioner of internal revenue (who administered the tobacco taxes) to take a hand as well.

In 1879 the union secured the support of Congressman Abram S. Hewitt, an iron manufacturer and a disciple of Peter Cooper, founder of Cooper Union. Steered by Hewitt, the bill passed the House, but failed in the Senate. The union then carried its efforts to the state legislature. Gompers and Strasser took turns riding the Hudson River boats to Albany to maintain a perpetual lobby. The union urged its members to vote for sympathetic candidates in the state elections of 1881, a case, Gompers said, not of party politics, but of "labor politics, pure and simple."

In order to collect compelling evidence of tenement-house abuse, Gompers made a survey of the tenements, masquerading as a book salesman armed with a set of Dickens. "Knowing the financial and cultural conditions of the Bohemian tenements," he recalled, "I knew I would not be embarrassed by making many sales." He found poverty, squalor, and disease, which he reduced to statistical tables and articles, hoping they would rouse the indignation of the public and its elected representatives. He realized, however, that evidence of degradation, however massive, did not guarantee a satisfactory political response, especially since some of the profits of exploitation found their way, by one means or another, into the pockets of politicians.

Getting the appropriate law enacted required forcing "home upon the 'consciences' of politicians the importance of legislation to abolish tenements." In his lobbying, Gompers showed he had learned much about the nature of American politics. He knew "that the conscience of the lawmakers resided in the ballot box" and that the way to "arouse [it] lay in the organized use of ballots." Thus the union's emergence as a political force in the elections of 1881 shows the "Americanization" of Sam Gompers and his determination to adapt tactics to the American milieu.

In his survey, Gompers made a discovery that heartened him: the tenement manufacturing system had declined appreciably as a result of the great strike. Gompers read this as evidence that he and his colleagues had created a viable organization and had put it on the road to success. He carried these conclusions to the meetings of the Economical and Sociological Club, an informal study group consisting of Gompers, Strasser, Laurrell, and a few others, some of them more or less socialists of various types. The club considered ways and means to deal with the problems of the workers in America and served, Gompers said, as "a practical clearing agency in the development of trade union understanding." In the beginning, the possibilities covered virtually the whole range of strategical and organizational alternatives — socialism of various kinds, trade unions, currency reform, mass meetings, general strikes, and so on. As time passed, however, experience and the pragmatism of Strasser and Laurrell narrowed the group's considerations to trade unions of the type built by the New York cigarmakers. Through debate in the club and trial and error in the field, Gompers, his friends, and "trade unionism went through a process of Americanization."

In order to maximize the influence of such unions, the group decided early that the cigarmakers and similar organizations in other trades should affiliate, preferably on a national basis. In time, they hoped to link the American body to similar ones in other countries, creating an international federation of trade unions in which common interests would transcend national differences. But they began by trying to collect the unions of New York City under a single umbrella. Two such central bodies already existed, one English-speaking and one German-speaking. In addition to delegates from trade unions, both welcomed such "nonworkers" as college professors and professional agitators.

Since Gompers and his friends were as determined to exclude nonworkers from federations as they were to keep them out of unions, they decided to undermine the existing bodies rather than to join or unite them. They established, therefore, another "dual" organization, called the Amalgamated Trades and Labor Assembly. The Amalgamated accepted only bona fide trade unions; all delegates had to be working craftsmen. To broadcast the doctrine, the group got control of an old socialist newspaper, renamed it the *Labor Standard,* and nominated as editor one of their number, an ex-Irish nationalist turned socialist, J. P. McDonnell.

Gompers focused most of his efforts in the 1870s on his own union, but he clearly had more grandiose schemes in mind. While visiting Indianapolis to organize a cigar local, he told a friend that such work was "only incidental to my greater project. I predict that some day I will be able to form a federation of all labor organizations in the United States, and that of that federation I shall one day be president." The prediction proved accurate, but the process took some years. The Amalgamated Trades and Labor Assembly, handicapped by the depression and beset by its socialist opponents, accomplished little. An appeal from Gompers and his friends for national trade-union cooperation, published in the *National Labor Tribune,* evoked small response. In 1878, the Amalgamated Association of Iron and Steel Workers took the initiative, followed by the typographical union; both met similar apathy. It took an external threat to overcome internal inertia and to galvanize the trade unionists into coordinated action.

The external threat was a call in 1881 from the Knights of Industry, a secret society in Indiana, and from the Amalgamated Labor Union, made up of renegades from the Knights of Labor, for a conference in Terre Haute to establish an international amalgamated union. At the meeting, a majority of the delegates proposed an organization that would supplant both the trade unions and the Knights of Labor, then throw the whole weight of American workers into a campaign for currency reform. Alarmed and outnumbered, the handful of trade-union delegates withdrew, caucused, and concluded that they must set up a conference of their own.

When the ensuing meeting, the National Labor Congress, convened in Pittsburgh on November 15, 1881, 107 delegates attended, representing thirty trade unions with forty thousand members. Gompers appeared for the Cigarmakers' International. The congress was equally divided between the two groups threatened by the proposed international amalgamated union — the Knights of Labor and the trade unions. A struggle for control ensued during which Gompers, manipulating the scenario with his accustomed parliamentary skill, worked out a "compromise" method of representation assuring that trade unionists would control the new body, named the Federation of Organized Trades and Labor Unions. One of their number, John Jarrett of the steelworkers' union, became president. Gompers was chosen as vice-president and as chairman of the legislative committee. Chairman Gompers immediately rammed through a resolution designed to short-circuit any attempt to align the new body with any socialist political party. The resolution declared that no member of the committee should publicly endorse any political party, though he remained free to back individual candidates if he chose. The delegates set up an organizational structure patterned after the British Trade Union Congress, the only precedent then available. They then adjourned, went home, and looked to the future.

In later years, Gompers explained the Federation of Trades as a natural response to the revolution in American industry. Since employers were banding together for self-preservation, workers must do the same; the emergence of larger units of capital demanded the creation of larger labor bodies; national markets and national corporations had to be met with a national union. "Industrial development," he said, "is generally reflected in labor organizations."

This explanation, however, holds no water. Trade unions finally agreed to a national federation not because of threats from capitalists, but because other popular movements that unionists could not control threatened to destroy their organizations just as they began, at last, to make some progress. Few of the delegates at the National Labor Congress represented crafts threatened by the new industrial order. That menace lay largely in the future. In any case, manufacturers' associations, though potentially a noose for unions, proved in practice to be "ropes of sand" (in the words of John D. Rockefeller). There was always a Jay Gould or a Matthew Hutchinson around ready to sacrifice the theoretical benefits of unity to the immediate satisfaction of individualism or profits. In fact, the inability of manufacturers to cooperate voluntarily led directly to the development of trusts like Standard Oil and the merger of small firms into huge corporations. When these structures emerged, they turned their fire on organized labor with devastating effect; but in 1881 the attack was yet to come.

Eighteen eighty-one, moreover, was a time of prosperity following the long depression of 1873–1879. For most craft-union members it was a time of relative labor scarcity, resulting in steady employment and improving wages. In such times, blacklists of unionists usually became inoperative; they got mislaid in the rush of business or burned in the fires of greed. Gompers and his allies thus waged a campaign to defend ground already held. Convinced that they had developed, through years of struggle and sacrifice, the organization needed to deal with employers, they now defended it against its rivals, the Knights of Labor and the socialists. This contest continued for many years.

I V

Politics Fail,
Socialists Rail,
and Patent Remedies
Cure Nothing
1881–1886

GOMPERS'S ROLE in the Federation of Trades signified the expanding scope of his ambitions. The principal focus of his activities, however, remained the cigarmakers' union in New York. In 1881 he thought that their recent progress at the bargaining table, in organizing drives, and in politics were harbingers of even better things to come.

Events soon proved his optimism premature. Reform legislation, painfully extracted from lawmakers, was swiftly thrown out by courts, nullifying years of effort. The socialists added to Gompers's woes, attacking his program and his leadership, and launching a divisive campaign for control of the New York local of the Cigarmakers' International. What had been a philosophical difference ripened into a running battle, as Gompers fought to keep the trade-union movement aligned with his plan and the socialists struggled to incorporate it into their own. Tough, resilient, and determined, Gompers abandoned politics, pushed the socialists aside, and scorned crackpot remedies in favor of the one effective weapon that labor alone controlled, direct action against employers.

The 1880s brought him challenges greater than any he had faced before, but in 1881 Gompers thought he had ample reasons for confidence. The growing solidarity and discipline within his own union had brought success in its negotiations with employers. The Federation of Trades seemed the first promising step toward an effective, national alliance of trade unions. The cohesiveness demonstrated by cigar workers, skilled and unskilled alike, during the strike of 1877 augured well for the ability of trade unions to organize all workers in the future. Gompers himself reflected the confidence of the time, advocating the unionization of all working people, regardless of sex, color, or degree of skill. His own reputation was growing steadily not only in the ranks of trade-union leaders but among employers and the public as well. His name appeared often in the newspapers, and he enjoyed notoriety as the subject of several editorial cartoons.

In this sanguine mood, he led labor into the battle for legislation to prohibit cigar manufacture in tenement houses. In the fall of 1881, labor supported the reelection of Edward Grosse, a former member of the typographical union, to the New York State legislature. Grosse's anti-tenement-house bill passed the state senate in early 1882. When the bill came up for consideration in the assembly, the official copy of it could not be found in the clerk's files; opponents had stolen it. This piracy, typical of the guerrilla warfare carried on amid the freewheeling corruption of state politics, occurred in the final hours of the legislature's session, and effectively postponed action until the next session.

When the legislature reconvened, passage of the bill seemed assured. Not only were three trade unionists members of the assembly, but Gompers had recruited a powerful ally in the person of a young aristocrat on the make, Theodore Roosevelt. Roosevelt, serving his second term in the assembly, was ap-

pointed to a committee to investigate tenement-house conditions. Gompers, who was well acquainted with the territory,
took Roosevelt on a tour of the area. Roosevelt knew a
popular issue when he smelled one and threw his support
behind the bill, which passed overwhelmingly and was signed
by Governor Grover Cleveland.

A "jubilee demonstration" to celebrate the victory proved
premature. Labor soon learned that "securing the enactment
of a law does not mean the solution of the problem." The
cigar manufacturers at once appealed to the courts, arguing
that the laws restricted personal liberty and the rights of
private property and that they contravened the Constitution
by impairing the obligation of valid contracts between employers and workers. Finally, the manufacturers claimed that
the measure's legal justification — the regulation of public
health — exceeded the legitimate police powers of the state.
The New York Court of Appeals accepted this argument and
threw out the law.

In 1884 labor secured the passage of a new bill, designed to
meet judicial objections. The battle resumed, but with the
same outcome; this time the court declared that the bill deprived labor of its right to work where, when, and how it
chose. The appeals court agreed that the law restricted liberty
and property and added that depriving people of the right to
work in their residences interfered with the "hallowed" influence of the "home." Here indeed the court struck a shattering blow to labor's future hopes, though Gompers did not
fully realize its implications at the time. He did learn that
"the power of the courts to pass upon constitutionality of law
so complicates reform by legislation as to seriously restrict the
effectiveness of that method."

After some debate the cigarmakers' union decided to abandon the legal struggle and to harass "the manufacturers by
strikes and agitation until they were convinced . . . that it
would be less costly for them to abandon the tenement manufacturing system and carry on the industry in factories under

decent conditions." In time this campaign succeeded, but Gompers deluded himself in thinking that the union's strategies forced the tobacco trade from the tenements into factories. The shift, when it came, resulted more from the mechanization of the industry than from pressure by labor. To maximize the savings in cost, machines had to be collected under a single roof, not scattered through the alleys of the city.

Gompers's disillusionment with the legal process proved expensive. As time passed, labor shifted its attack more and more into the economic arena, employing the weapons of strikes and boycotts. Capital, however, repulsed the assault and counterattacked in the legislatures and in the courts, arguing successfully that collective bargaining (in which chosen delegates negotiated terms of employment for all workers in a shop or craft), strikes, and boycotts restricted property rights, the individual rights of workers, and the contract rights of everyone.

The arguments with which the courts struck down the anti-tenement laws exhibited the traditional American attitudes toward individual liberty, toward the rights of property, and toward the desirability of minimal governmental interference with either. The decisions, moreover, characterized the prevailing feeling that individual and property rights were inextricably intermingled. Under the controlling mentality, a decision which argued that property must be restricted so that individuals could be safeguarded would have seemed topsy-turvy logic. The idea lay far in the future that when human rights and property rights were antagonistic, human considerations should prevail.

To some extent the alliance between courts and capital resulted from the political corruption of the times. Judges were notoriously for sale to the highest bidder, particularly in New York, and labor's poverty gave it little chance at the auction. While the Drews, the Goulds, the Vanderbilts, and their rival buccaneers converted the halls of justice into burlesque theatres, labor could do little but watch the show.

Often their own attorneys betrayed labor's interests, as Strasser found to his sorrow when he hired Roscoe Conkling to represent the cigarmakers in the court battle over the antitenement law.

But corruption only partially explained the courts' defense of property as a bulwark of individual liberty. The idea had firm roots in the Anglo-American legal tradition. British parliaments over the centuries had enacted laws that adapted the protections enumerated in Magna Carta to changing conditions. The United States inherited the spirit of these laws. In a country where property holding was widespread, protection of property rights concerned many, not just the wealthy, and this concern was codified in several provisions of the Constitution. These provisions contemplated situations in which the protagonists would be the state and the individual; therefore, the yoking of property and human rights seemed logical and necessary. The emergence of huge accumulations of wealth vastly complicated things. Industrialization accelerated the creation of wealth. The rise of ever larger firms, increasingly held by corporations rather than individuals, concentrated more and more property in fewer and fewer hands.

In the late nineteenth century it became increasingly clear that concentration of wealth created a situation for which there was little precedent. Rich and poor no longer shared the same interests, even if both owned property. Equal protection under the law produced unequal results. The chief threat to the liberties of the people no longer lay in the potential tyrannies of government but in the real abuses of wealth and power, abuses committed in the sacred name of both individual and property rights. Consequently, the late nineteenth century saw the emergence of popular protests by labor as well as by farmers and small businessmen. When these uprisings produced laws to protect the weak against the strong, they were contested in the courts, which almost invariably struck them down. The judges so acted not only because they had been bought, but because it was far from clear how to defend the rights of some by limiting the same rights of others. Even those who agreed that wealth must somehow be curbed disagreed on how to do it without causing more harm than good.

Many felt that industrialization must be stopped, or even reversed, so that America could return to its happier (if somewhat mythical) past, in which artisans and yeoman farmers dominated. Gompers, his friends, and even their socialist enemies never fell for this silliness: Marx had taught them better. Industrialization resulted from an inevitable historical process; and history could not be reversed.

Gompers accepted the logic of industrialization. The trade unions' role, as he saw it, was not to waste time trying to stop the process but to see that workers shared its benefits and escaped its abuses. Concluding that the legal process offered no hope for the workers' cause, he largely withdrew from the legislatures that made it and the courts that interpreted it and took the labor movement with him. Withdrawal did not mean civil disobedience. With a few exceptions he accepted the law and urged his followers to obey it. He opposed violence on picket lines, for example, and always argued that contracts, once made, must be upheld by labor as well as by management. If he found a statute intolerable, he would fight it in the courts, but he accepted the court's final decision, even when it meant emasculating his movement. He thus demonstrated his adherence to the fundamental American belief in the rule of law, and he waged his battles with the dwindling stock of weapons left him by hostile court decisions. Most of his followers, sharing his view, supported his policy.

In forgoing political solutions for economic ones, Gompers made some short-run progress but uncoupled the labor movement from the locomotive of history. In the United States, politics remained the ultimate locus of power, and Americans, for all their faith in the business system, still retained their trust in law as the final arbiter of human affairs. Since the country's foundation, the dominant philosophy had argued that the solution to all society's problems lay in the creation and proper administration of the appropriate form of government. When the political principles governing the United States encouraged the transition of a nation of artisans and farmers into a complex industrial society and the protection of individual rights broke down, the disenchanted could choose only from the philosophical remedies at hand. In the economic sphere, the theoretical alternatives that had appeared by the late nineteenth century were the various forms of socialism and a satchel full of patent medicines whose principal ingredient was some kind of reform of the monetary system.

Socialism appealed to few because it involved the abolition or restriction of private property, and Americans wanted not to eliminate property but to protect what they had and to preserve a fair chance to acquire more. The best way to do this, it seemed, was to use the political process to modify the rules so that the new industrial game produced the old democratic outcome, and to use the government in its traditional role as referee.

The public's willingness to rely on the political system eventuated in legislation — much of it passed during the AF of L's first thirty years — that created agencies to regulate trusts and monopolies, interstate transportation, the quality of food and drugs, and abuses of big business. Insofar as these laws accepted the inevitability of industrialization and aimed at maximizing its benefits and minimizing its abuses, the prevailing reform philosophy resembled Gompers's own views. In time, the process of reform added laws that made organized labor a powerful force, but because of Gompers's tactics labor played little role in the movement.

By withdrawing labor as an organized force from the political arena for twenty years, Gompers discarded its most powerful potential weapon. His alternative plan, direct economic action against employers, proved inadequate to the challenges posed by industrialization. Although he realistically accepted the inevitability of the factory system and the huge corporations that grew out of it, he never devised a practical counter-thrust to protect industrial workers. The AF of L succeeded to the extent it did because Gompers increasingly concentrated on promoting the welfare of the workers least affected by the new methods of production. Even for this fortunate minority, direct economic action waned in effectiveness against employers who fought not on the picket lines, but in the courts.

Before retiring from the political fray, Gompers had one last fling at reform through the ballot box. He supported Henry George for mayor of New York in the fall campaign of 1886. George's book, *Progress and Poverty,* diagnosed the social ills accompanying industrialization as natural consequences of capital's tightening control on land. The value of land increased through the progress of society as a whole, but the wealth thus created did not benefit all the people, only the few who controlled the real estate. As they grew richer, they bought more land, grew even richer, and so on. George's remedy was a panacea called the "single tax," which would confiscate the "unearned increment" created by rising land values and return it to society. His plan attracted a considerable following in 1886. The idea of a simple solution for such complex problems appealed to many.

In addition, George raised several issues about which Americans had long been sensitive. The ready availability of land, for example, had played such a major role in the development of American attitudes that the prospect of monopolistic control was a frightening specter, especially in an era when the closure of the once endless frontier seemed imminent. George, furthermore, did not advocate radical reform. His plan did not involve the elimination of property but instead proposed a method of harnessing private enterprise more effectively to society's needs. Nor did he espouse extralegal means; he worked within the system. George hoped to attract a large enough following at the ballot box to enact the single tax through the traditional legislative process. George's campaign attracted a broad spectrum of Americans who wanted reform through legislation and were willing to support a third party to get it. Among this group, workingmen formed a potentially sizable contingent.

Unfortunately for George's backers, there were several powerful reasons why a third party had little prospect of building a successful coalition. Industrial capitalism, far from contradicting the tenets of private property, mobility, and law, grew naturally out of them. Since these beliefs formed a common ground shared by most American voters, the major political parties, reflecting the majority view, bunched close together in the middle. No third party had a hope of building an alternative platform in the center where most of the votes lay; they had to nibble at the fringes where issues abounded but voters were few.

The structure of the American political system compounded the difficulty. In some countries each party wins legislative representation proportionate to its share of the total popular vote. Where such a system prevails, a third party sometimes exerts a disproportionately powerful leverage by exacting major concessions in return for forming a coalition with one of the larger parties. These concessions are used to attract more voters, win more seats, and so on. In the United States, however, each political district elects only one member at each election. The winner takes all and the loser gets nothing. In American politics, therefore, nothing could be accomplished with a small following — only a plurality would do. Consequently, success depended on building a winning coalition by finding a philosophy under which disparate groups could unite, or by seizing on new issues compelling enough to draw voters from the old parties to a new one.

The socialists repeatedly tried the former tactic, but their philosophy, certainly an alternative to the one embraced by Republicans and Democrats, drew only a handful. Other third parties — Greenback-labor and Populist, for example — found attractive issues from time to time, but long before they could obtain a majority (except in isolated localities), the major parties demolished the newcomers by usurping their issues.

In the years before George's campaign, alliances between labor and third parties had failed conspicuously. In 1872, the National Labor Union had set up the National Labor Reform party, nominated a candidate for president, and then expired because of political ineptitude, a lack of funds, and internal dissension. In 1876 the Greenback party nominated Peter Cooper for president, but the expected heavy support from labor never materialized. The wave of strikes in 1877 rekindled the Greenback-labor alliance, and the party ran presidential candidates in 1880 (James B. Weaver) and 1884 (Benjamin F. Butler). Neither campaign yielded much at the polls: 3.4 percent and 1.8 percent of the popular vote.

All these parties had in common a reliance on a central issue, the expansion of the money supply by issuing paper currency, and like George with the single tax, offered a simplistic nostrum for complex ailments. The dominant monetary theory of the times argued that paper money's value depended on its redeemability in gold. People used paper notes with confidence, knowing they could get gold for them any time they chose. The original issuance of greenbacks during the Civil War was justified as an emergency measure, and it won congressional approval only with the stipulation that greenbacks be withdrawn as soon as possible after the war. In the post–Civil War period, the question of greenback retirement became a major political issue, particularly among those who needed easy credit and found it hard to obtain. Farmers, small businessmen, and nostalgists who yearned for a return to an America of individual enterprise not only wanted existing greenbacks kept in circulation but wanted more printed, making it easier for them to borrow. In addition, they feared (with some justification) that the country's population and economy would expand faster than the gold supply, making gold increasingly valuable, harder for the poor to get, and easier for the wealthy to monopolize.

Greenback parties, like most other third parties, never made much progress, partly because powerful voices among capitalists and theorists argued the opposing case, and partly because much of the electorate distrusted such cure-alls and their zany proponents. Gompers was one of the skeptics. Although he voted for the Greenback candidates in 1880 and 1884, he did so more as a protest against the major parties than as a gesture of faith in the Greenback program. He had no confidence in such simple solutions. "Labor's ills cannot be cured by patent medicine," he said, and the fate of the antitenement campaign did nothing to ease his pessimistic view of the political process.

The wave of popular support for George's candidacy, however, swept Gompers up in spite of his reservations. At first he declined to involve himself; such efforts in the past had wasted time and energies better devoted to more practical causes. He said that "John Swinton [editor of a labor newspaper] . . . and others . . . might give some reminiscences to our friends who are anxious for workingmen to rush into politics." Swinton himself, however, helped persuade Gompers to change his mind. "Never mind reviews, Brother Gompers," Swinton said. "Let the dead past bury the dead. . . . Today is not yesterday and tomorrow will be different from both."

Those were probably not the deciding arguments from Gompers, however. Politician himself, though he decried politics, Gompers realized that George's campaign had excited a considerable following among labor. Ever attuned to the mood of his constituency, he shifted ground and took to the stump in George's behalf. Although only five feet four, Gompers had a powerful build and a strong countenance (enriched by a dark handlebar mustache) and he made a commanding presence on a speaker's platform. His days of stammering uncertainty had long passed; he had learned how to arouse a crowd. He was charismatic and had a stentorian voice that could be heard three city blocks away without a microphone. All these assets he threw into the battle against George's opponents, Theodore Roosevelt (Republican) and Abram Hewitt (Democrat).

With his usual energy he circulated throughout the city, speaking by day and by night, and wrote articles for labor papers. Yet, despite all this effort, George lost to Hewitt. Many of George's supporters rallied round him in defeat and launched a campaign for the governorship the following year.

But not Gompers. He had had enough of party politics. He regretted his "curious determination to disregard experience" and vowed not to repeat it. In subsequent years he kept himself and the AF of L out of third-party movements and focused on immediate economic gains. "The labor movement, to succeed politically," he declared, "must work for present and tangible results. While keeping in view a lofty ideal, we must advance towards it through practical steps, taken with intelligent regard for pressing needs." Individual workers could and should vote for sympathetic candidates, he believed, but organized labor should keep clear of political parties and neither try to form one of its own nor endorse any existing one. In this way labor would not dissipate its energies in useless causes, but instead could exert continuous pressure for immediate economic improvements in the workplace, thus making more progress than by "dabbling in that cesspool of corruption commonly known as party politics." Gompers maintained this position for twenty years. Under his dominance, the AF of L maintained a "masterly inactivity" until 1906, when business's successful legal campaigns forced him to venture once more into the political field. By that time he could do but little, and it came too late.

In the meantime, Gompers's political activities had involved him in open warfare with increasingly virulent enemies, the socialists. Against them he could not follow a policy of withdrawal. Instead, he mounted a ruthless attack to force them either into compliance with his policies or out of the labor movement altogether. The first open rupture came in 1881, when the cigarmakers' union endorsed sympathetic candidates in the state election. A few hard-core socialists left the union in protest, claiming that labor owed allegiance to one party only, the Socialist Labor Party; supporting any others delayed the development of class consciousness by making workers think that collaboration with the establishment could bring progress. Many socialists who remained in the union also decried the policy of endorsement and lobbying, because hobnobbing with politicos exposed labor leaders to the temptations of bribes and political appointments betraying the workers' cause.

This dispute opened within the union ranks a rift that widened on the issue of raising dues and that became a gulf as a result of Local 144's presidential election in 1882. The members elected a socialist slate that included Samuel Schimkowitz as president. Ten members protested on the grounds that Schimkowitz was an employer and therefore ineligible. Strasser, by this time bitterly antisocialist, promptly threw out the results. A Byzantine struggle then dragged out over the next two years. Strasser consistently declined to certify any investigation upholding the socialists' claims. Despairing of justice through the established process, the socialists seceded from the Cigarmakers' International and formed their own union, thus making it possible for employers to play one faction against the other to the detriment of both.

Gompers never forgave the defectors. His distaste for socialist methods hardened into hatred. To socialists, he believed, the party was "a fetish"; "rule or ruin" the union was their motto. Since the socialist faction may well have had a majority within Local 144, at least for a time, Strasser and Gompers practiced a little rule or ruin of their own. In addition, they temporarily set democracy aside and accepted the creation of an anathematic dual union, both steps they denounced in others.

Gompers argued that the end justified the means; the trade union had to be preserved at all costs against a movement whose folly would arouse popular antagonism and nullify progress. "The trade union is not a Sunday School," he reflected. When threatened, he willingly fell back on tactics that smacked more of the street fighter than of a dedicated democrat. Moreover, personal resentment reinforced his conviction that his policy and Strasser's would build a strong labor movement and that the socialists' methods would be "hari-kari." During the struggle, their enemies denounced Gompers and Strasser as "unscrupulous leaders who appealed to passion and hatred, whose only ambition was self-aggrandizement, who aspired to both national and local fame, who stooped to every known method of fraud and deception to accomplish their own nefarious ends."

This attack, some of it near enough to the mark, aroused Gompers's fighting blood more effectively than mere doctrinal disputes ever could. He proved to be a good hater; he never forgave. In the years that followed the schism of 1883, he continued from time to time to use socialist rhetoric and to claim that he differed from the socialists only in means not ends. But, in fact, he moved steadily away from the radical flirtations of his youth, beating back socialist attempts to control the leadership and the policies of the AF of L. In 1903, he felt sure enough of his position to denounce the socialists publicly: "Their statements as to economic ills are right. Their conclusions and their philosophy are all askew." Addressing them directly, he added:

I want to tell you, Socialists, that I have studied your philosophy; read your works upon economics, and not the meanest of them; studied your standard works, both in English and German — have not only read, but studied them. I have heard your orators and watched the work of your movement the world over. I have kept close watch upon your doctrines for thirty years; have been closely associated with many of you, and know how you think and what you propose. I know, too, what you have up your sleeve. And I want to say to you that I am entirely at variance with your philosophy. . . . Economically, you are unsound; socially, you are wrong; industrially, you are an impossibility.

Whatever the precise balance of experience, instinct, historical observation, self-interest, and hate that induced Gompers to turn away from socialism, the alienation became total.

It also worked to his advantage, for although by rejecting the political process he failed to back the right horse in the American derby, by rejecting socialism he refused to bet on the wrong one. Socialism may have been popular among the New York cigarmakers in 1881, but it ran head-on into the dominant values in America as a whole and made little progress against them.

Few American workers exhibited class consciousness. They rarely responded to appeals from labor parties, "else every city in America would be ruled by workingmen," as one socialist lamented in 1886. The backbone of most third parties in the late nineteenth century, from Greenback to Populist, was not labor but small farmers whose mentality was petit bourgeois rather than proletarian.

In the American environment, labor failed to develop class consciousness even in the late nineteenth century, when the headlong industrialization of the economy created a situation that was, theoretically at least, a Marxian delight. Instead, workers, despite their disparate backgrounds, retained their common attachment to mobility, property, and the capitalist system that provided both. Marx himself recognized the obstacles to the development of a permanent proletariat in America, noting in 1865 "the continuous conversion of wages labourers into independent, self-sustaining peasants." In such conditions of mobility, Marx observed, "the function of a wages labourer is for a very large part of the American people but a probational state, which they are sure to leave within a longer or shorter term." Marx's American contemporary, Abraham Lincoln, made a similar observation.

Time did not weaken the workingman's attachment to mobility, property, and capitalism. In 1877, Gompers's associate, J. P. McDonnell, noted that annihilating "the power of capitalism in Europe" was "comparatively easy . . . because the disinherited class cannot hope to rise beyond their accustomed level, and capitalism is hateful to them from times immemorial." In the United States, on the other hand,

McDonnell declared, capitalism "resides in the breast of almost everybody."

Sometimes the labor movement itself provided the means for workers "to rise beyond their accustomed level." Gompers witnessed the defection of many labor leaders "who, having grown to some degree of prominence and having demonstrated their ability to serve their fellows . . . had been elected or appointed to public offices . . . entered business, [or] accepted positions as foremen or superintendents." Although Gompers himself rejected many such offers, he certainly exuded ambition, used the labor movement as a vehicle to drive himself forward, enjoyed his familiarity with influential politicians and businessmen, and registered his deep satisfaction in fulfilling the traditional American goal of owning a home. When he bought a house, he said he was "at last free to gratify an intense desire that [he] had had since childhood . . . a real house surrounded by trees and grounds where flowers could grow and where [he] could watch the birds and hear them sing."

In other ways Gompers exhibited the enduring American faith in mobility. His whole program of economic improvement aimed at elevating the living conditions of American workers to the point where they enjoyed the same amenities as the country's middle class. He believed too in upward mobility from generation to generation: "Children of employees should be kept from factories, workhouses, and mines." This would enable them to stay in school, and, through education, "our children should be superior to the present generation." He tried to follow this policy within his own family. "[We] wanted our children to have opportunities denied us, and sent them to school as long as we could."

Gompers recognized that industrialization involved the permanent existence of a large number of workers who labored for others in return for wages. But he did not assume that people who manned the factories at any particular time were condemned to do so forever or that children would follow in their parents' footsteps. Gompers observed a process of mobility in which many workers, and even more workers' children, departed the factory for some other way of life or moved from the ranks of labor into supervisory positions. Immigration provided the manpower to take their places.

Gompers himself took part in the same movement. He often claimed that he remained a worker all his life, but obviously he did not. He left the factory and became a middle-class bureaucrat. The trade-union movement, he believed, could preserve the individual factory worker's self-respect and independence while he reaped the benefits of industrial prosperity. These views were self-serving in that they reflected his own ambitions. But they also embodied conclusions drawn from his experiences in the early 1880s: politics offered only empty promises; socialism offered only useless doctrine. Both consumed the workers' energies and gave nothing in return. Having tried both in the past, Gompers was determined to steer clear of them in the future.

V

In the Days
of the Knights
the AF of L Is Born

1881–1886

I N THE EARLY 1880s, while learning the hard lessons
of politics and battling the socialists, Gompers tackled an
additional foe, the Knights of Labor. The Knights, originally
founded in 1869 as a secret society of workingmen, gradually
abandoned secrecy, expanded after the collapse of the National
Labor Union in 1873, and emerged as a potential force in
America in the late 1870s. Gompers and his colleagues watched
its growth with a suspicion that ripened into hostility. In 1886
the Knights so threatened the preeminence of trade unions in
organized labor that Gompers helped junk the enfeebled
Federation of Organized Trades and Labor Unions and
joined those who replaced it with a leaner, harder instrument,
the American Federation of Labor. With the new weapon he
engaged the Knights in a battle to the death.

By rejecting political action and socialism, Gompers had
narrowed the range of alternative labor strategies to strikes
and boycotts, had limited the participants to bona fide workers, and had jettisoned long-range programs of social realign-
ment in favor of immediate improvements in wages, hours,

and working conditions. These moves placed him squarely at odds with the Knights, as did his acceptance of the realities of evolving industrial America with an economy made up of profit-seeking employers and wage-earning employees.

The Knights, in contrast, opposed strikes and boycotts until rank-and-file pressure forced the leadership into a grudging acceptance of such tactics. Even then the "Master Workman" and guiding spirit of the Knights, Terence V. Powderly, retained his personal preference for arbitration as a means of settling industrial disputes. The strike, Powderly declared, was a "relic of barbarism" and "productive of more injury than benefit to working people."

Unlike Gompers's organizations, the Knights welcomed members from all walks of life except the "parasitic" professions of gambling, stockbrokerage, law, banking (all regarded as fundamentally the same), and the manufacture or sale of intoxicating beverages. Employers and employees alike were accepted because the Knights intended to remake American society in a way that would eradicate the distinction. "The aim of the Knights of Labor — properly understood — is to make each man his own employer," Powderly declared. Making every man his own boss involved stopping the march of the economy toward industrialization and putting it on the road back to a society made up of small independent producers.

In industries where such small producing units could not function, Powderly proposed to replace profit-making firms, whether individually or corporately owned, with producers' cooperatives in which all participants shared the proceeds. Above all, Powderly's economic utopia would eliminate the very element on which Gompers hoped to exert organized labor's most potent pressure, wages.

To these differences, sufficient in themselves to put the Knights and the trade unions on a collision course, were added the exacerbating conflicts of background and attitudes between the men at the helms. Most of the trade unions' leadership consisted of European immigrants; native-born Americans dominated the Knights. Trade-union rhetoric, borrowed from socialism, emphasized the struggle between the employing and the working classes. Gompers, for example, often made such statements as, "There are two classes in society, one incessantly striving to obtain the labor of the other class for as little as possible." Powderly on the other hand declared, "I hate the word 'class' and would drive it from the English language if I could." The Knights favored more traditional American language of protest. Their proclamations often paraphrased documents such as the Declaration of Independence and the Constitution. Powderly, a devout Catholic, called Gompers, a nonpracticing Jew, a "Christslugger." Powderly, who did not drink, publicly referred to Gompers, for whom the saloon was the workingman's clubhouse and a natural habitat, as a drunk. That kind of attack as many socialists could testify, made Gompers an implacable enemy. Long after the Knights had expired, Gompers showed that he retained his personal animosity by declining to support Powderly's application for a political appointment under Theodore Roosevelt.

The Knights of Labor's emergence as an organizer of rival trade unions escalated hostility into all-out war between Gompers and the Knights. This development, largely coterminous with the life span of the Federation of Trades (1881–1886), threatened to supplant Gompers's organization as the guiding force in the American trade-union movement and to thwart his personal ambition to lead it. Powderly's ideal structure for the Knights consisted of bodies called local assemblies, which enrolled all comers (except the few specifically disqualified), educated them, and organized them to work for "a radical change in the existing industrial system." These mixed local assemblies were grouped into district assemblies. Such heterogeneous bodies could not have functioned as industrial bargaining units and were not intended for that purpose. The mixed assemblies, therefore, presented little threat to the existing trade unions; in fact, the Federation of Trades permitted district assemblies to send delegates to its annual convention, and many trade-union leaders also belonged to the Knights.

From the outset, however, the Knights included many dedicated trade unionists who rejected Powderly's organizational philosophy. They won his grudging assent to their demand for admission of local assemblies consisting of members from a single trade. Trade assemblies always made up a large proportion of the total, and their number expanded after the strikes of 1877 as the Knights, despite the reservations of much of the leadership, became a militant labor organization. Many trade unionists joined the Knights; sometimes whole locals enrolled in a body. Gompers observed this process with dismay. Each craft union that affiliated with the Knights represented one less potential addition to the Federation of Trades; moreover, they diminished labor's chances for progress by casting their lot with the Knights' unrealistic reform philosophy.

Although Gompers deeply resented the Knights' threat to his plans and his prominence, he could scarcely object on principle when trade unions freely chose to join a rival body. He soon gained allies, however. The Knights, not content with annexing existing unions, began committing the sin of dual unionism. By the early 1880s, most of the unions in America held this grievance against the Knights. Between 1880 and 1886, this antagonism mushroomed, along with the Knights' membership, which rose from a few thousand to seven hundred thousand. The Knights particularly enraged Gompers by embroiling themselves in the row between the factions of the cigarmakers' Local 144 and by refusing to concede to his demands that they cease engaging in dual unionism. When the socialist rebels seceded from Gompers's local in New York, they found a new home among the Knights. The New York branch of the Knights, District Assembly 49, was a particularly militant one, and it encouraged the defectors. Backed by the Knights, the socialist group competed vigorously with Gompers's Local 144 for members and contracts. In those days it was the custom for union-made cigars to bear a distinctive label; Local 144's was blue. The Knights established a rival white label of their own.

In time the socialist cigarmakers and the Knights parted company. They had little in common but their enemy, Gompers, and the Knights' prevailing (though often internally disputed) philosophy differed even more from the socialists' than did the trade unions'. The alliance lasted long enough, however, to justify open warfare. Seeing a chance to shatter both hated rivals with a single blow, Sam pursued the battle with his customary ruthlessness. He and his colleagues formed the Defiance Assembly and joined the Knights for the sole purpose of getting a supply of the white labels so that Local 144's cigars could sport two union labels instead of one. When the Knights' cigarmakers went on strike, Gompers's local supplied strikebreakers (scabs) to the embattled employers. Now and again treaties of peace were offered and rejected or accepted and broken by one side or the other. As Gompers grew more confident of his tactics and his organization, he demanded ever more stringent terms; by 1886 he wanted little less than unconditional surrender from his rivals in New York.

In the same year, he mounted a campaign to undermine the Knights' national preeminence in the labor movement. He prodded the moribund Federation of Trades into a fresh attack for an eight-hour day. The federation urged its members to demand a shorter workday and then participate in a general strike on May 1 should the demand be rejected. Designed largely as a publicity stunt to enhance the prestige of the federation, the eight-hour campaign precipitated events that proved devastating to the Knights. Powderly reluctantly endorsed the plan (he could scarcely have done otherwise without alienating many of his followers and playing into Gompers's hand), but privately advised the assemblies not to participate in a general strike.

Gompers went to Chicago and spoke in Union Square on May 1. Tempers in the area already ran high. A long strike at the International Harvester plant, one of Chicago's largest employers, had recently been broken by scab labor protected by Chicago police and a force of security guards supplied by the Pinkerton Detective Agency.

Chicago on May 1, 1886, juxtaposed elements of labor's past and future. While Gompers rallied the city's trade unionists against their employers, the dispossessed Harvester workers gathered near the plant on the outskirts of town and debated ways to grapple with their potent corporate enemy. Gompers's followers and the small shops where most of them worked were relics of the preindustrial past. International Harvester and its antilabor tactics were harbingers of an ominous future for labor. Small-scale employers, heavily dependent on skilled labor, generally conceded the right of their workers to belong to unions. Ordinarily, such employers either negotiated with their workers, often drawing out the negotiations for as long as possible, or rejected all proposals and tried to nullify labor's weapons by seeking legal means to prevent strikes and boycotts. The central issue was usually the simple one of money. Whether the workers demanded more pay, shorter hours, or better conditions, shop owners translated these into a matter of cost. They rarely disputed their employees' right to make such demands or to present them through their unions. Negotiations were often tempered by personal relationships. Employers and employees usually were well acquainted with each other. By 1886, for example, Gompers had known most of New York's cigar manufacturers, like Stachelburg and Hirsch, for twenty years.

Trade-union progress came largely in industries dominated by owner-managers who treated labor's demands as a matter of cost, not power. Proprietors enjoyed the security of power provided by ownership, though labor costs directly and immediately affected their own welfare. To negotiate might eventually result in diminished profits, but a strike meant the certain and immediate loss of all income. Until they found legal ways to nullify labor's tactics by preventing strikes and boycotts, such employers were inclined to negotiate. Consequently, Gompers's eight-hour movement, resumed in 1886, achieved some success in trades like his own and the carpenters'.

Corporations like International Harvester were another matter. Harvester was a trust formed by the merger of several firms in the farm-implement industry. Its day-to-day affairs were managed not by its stockholder-proprietors, but by a salaried bureaucratic staff, which often regarded the very existence of a union as a challenge to its right to manage — in other words, as a negation of a fundamental property right. Unions raised an issue more basic than that of money, the issue of management's inherent power to direct the company's affairs in any legal way. The managers responded by trying first to eradicate the union by discharging employees who belonged. If this failed and the union called a strike, the corporation usually refused to negotiate and hired scabs, which they could do more easily than small shops because mechanized methods of production depended less on skilled labor. In addition, professional managers seldom knew their workers personally, so friendship rarely constrained them from discharging workers. To protect the strikebreakers against violence from strikers, firms called upon the community's resources to safeguard private property. Just as the railroads had enlisted the aid of sheriffs and militia in 1877, so the Chicago police responded to Harvester's pleas in 1886.

In the years after 1886, Harvester's modern labor tactics confronted workers increasingly as corporate employers made unionization an issue of power threatening professional managers much more than did financial demands. Since executives worked for salaries, the outcome of wage negotiations had little direct effect on their own fortunes, but their sense of self-importance depended on unquestioned authority over employees' conduct. When this authority came under attack, they defended themselves vigorously, violently if need be, with the aid of Pinkertons and similar auxiliaries.

Gompers soon felt the consequences of the new corporate style of labor relations, for the death knell of the Federation of Trades was sounded by a clash that took place in Chicago at the same time as his rally. On May 3, a crowd of striking Harvester workers attacked a group of scabs outside the plant. The police counterattacked, killing or wounding six strikers. The unions organized a mass meeting for the following evening in Haymarket Square to protest police brutality. Some four thousand people gathered on the rain-slicked cobblestones and stood sullen but peaceful in the glare of the gaslights and the flickering torches to hear the speakers. Such gatherings rarely achieved concrete results, but served to vent frustrations harmlessly, particularly if left alone by the police.

This time, the mayor (who attended the meeting) and the police force got their signals crossed. At the end of the evening, rain began to fall heavily, and the crowd started to disperse. The police decided to hurry the process, ordered the speaker to desist, and began hustling the crowd out of the square. An argument erupted. In the midst of it someone lobbed a bomb into a knot of policemen, killing one and wounding seventy more. The police fired into the crowd; the crowd fired back. In seconds the peaceful meeting became a bloody shambles. Ten people died and scores were injured.

The Haymarket Riot came at the end of ten years of labor unrest that opened with the Molly Maguire riots in 1875 and the violent railroad strikes in 1877. Waves of strikes in successive years, inflammatory rhetoric from socialists and anarchists, the rise of the Knights of Labor as a mass movement, all accompanied by occasional outbursts of violence, especially when strikebreakers appeared, produced a mood of near hysteria among the general public. To many Americans it looked as though there lurked in the ranks of labor a significant element ready for riot, sabotage, arson, pillage, and even murder.

The Haymarket bombing seemed to confirm the public's worst fears. It provoked a savage response. The police grabbed the first eight "anarchists" they could find and charged them with murder. The judge, the prosecutor, and an openly biased jury rammed through a guilty verdict though only three of the men had been in the square when the bomb was thrown. No one offered proof that any of them had thrown it or that the speakers had even advocated violence, let alone participated in any. The mayor described the speeches as "tame." Nevertheless, the judge justified the verdict on the grounds that

they had generally by speech and print advised large classes to commit murder and had left the commission, the time [and] place . . . to the individual will, whim or caprice . . . of each individual man who listened to their advice.

No officer of the Knights of Labor or of a trade union spoke at the Haymarket rally. Anarchism, moreover, played no part in the program of either. The public, however, convicted organized labor by implication. The Knights of Labor suffered most from the vindictive post-Haymarket mood. Its membership declined thereafter. To Gompers and his sympathizers, May 1886 presented a crisis. Beset by the dual unionism of the Knights and hampered at every turn by public hostility, they decided to act. Peter J. McGuire of the Brotherhood of Carpenters called for a conference of national trade unions in Philadelphia on May 17. Gompers recalled it as "the largest meeting of trade union executives I had attended up to that time." "It was," he said, "an impressive gathering of men of good presence and exceptional ability." It was also a collection of gentlemen proletarians ("practically every man wore a silk hat and a Prince Albert coat") representing traditional trades, including

William Weihe, six feet six, the giant puddler [a skill already fast disappearing in the blast furnaces at Carnegie's works]; Joseph Wilkinson, the handsome tailor; P. J. McGuire [of the carpenters], a lovable, genial companion [too much so; he died of alcoholism];

E. S. McIntosh of the International Typographers Union; Henry Emrich, the eloquent leader of the Furniture Workers; and Adolph Strasser, the Bismarck of the Cigarmakers.

And, of course, Gompers.

This group drafted a treaty of peace to be dictated to the next national gathering of the Knights of Labor. It demanded that the Knights disband all dual unions, refrain from establishing new ones, expel any member "who works for less than the regular scale of wages fixed by the union of his craft" or anyone "convicted of scabbing, ratting, embezzlement, or any other offense against the union of his trade." It also stipulated that the Knights would not permit their members to work in any shop struck by a trade union, nor would they establish "any trade mark or label in competition with any . . . now issued, or . . . issued [in the future] by any national or international trade union."

The document effectively demanded that the Knights of Labor withdraw from the labor movement entirely. Powderly rejected this ukase, compounding the felony in Gompers's eyes by a personal attack. "The unaccountable actions" of the trade-union officers, Powderly wrote, could only be explained by the fact that "men who indulge in excess . . . of intoxicants cannot transact business with cool heads. On two occasions the men who came to . . . confer with the Executive Board [of the Knights] were too full for utterance." In October, the General Assembly of the Knights rejected the agreement.

In November 1886, the Federation of Organized Trades and Labor Unions held its sixth and last meeting in Columbus, Ohio. The trade unionists, "convinced that the old Federation could not do the effective work required," scrapped the organization, created the American Federation of Labor, and elected a slate of officers that included Gompers as president with a salary of $1,000 a year. The AF of L was designed to fill the need "for a consolidated organization for the promotion of trade unionism [to] work . . . daily for the organization of all workers of America, skilled as well as unskilled." The new federation "needed a central office and officers who could give all their time to the Federation work." The AF of L abandoned the Federation of Trades' program of relief by legislation; its founders "revised [the Federation of Trades'] constitution to authorize work in the economic field."

Although his salary did not begin until the following March, Gompers set to work at once with a will, a plan, and little else. The first "central office" was a small room provided rent-free by the cigarmakers' Local 144 and was furnished with a box for a chair. The full-time staff consisted of Gompers and his son Henry, hired as office boy at three dollars a week. With this meager equipment, Gompers set out to make the AF of L "something more than a paper organization." He was "president of a Federation that had been created but had yet to be given vitality." His mission had a desperate urgency, for organized labor's fortunes were at low ebb. Only trade unions could revive them, Gompers believed, and "the trade union movement stood or fell with the success of the [new] Federation."

Gompers was thirty-seven years old and had been preparing all his life for the task of federation president. He "gave everything within [him] to the work." For Gompers, one of his colleagues observed, the AF of L became "the Father, the Son, and the Holy Ghost." He had little formal authority. The AF of L's constitution was patterned somewhat after the Constitution of the United States, but restricted the chief executive's powers to those of persuasion. To this limited commission, however, Gompers brought the potency of a well-developed gospel of labor, a potency backed by boundless energy, skill as a labor politician, a solid phalanx of dedicated supporters, and by a mixture of combativeness and patience. Above all, he had a plan, a pragmatic program distilled from the vapor of theory by trial and error. Labor must focus on immediate gains ("more, more, here and now"), must press its demands for higher wages, shorter hours, and better conditions through strikes and boycotts on selected targets at appropriate times. The proper structure to carry out this program was the trade union, organized by crafts and subdivided according to geography.

The AF of L and its strategies still did not represent a calculated response to industrialization. Instead, it was an instrument forged in the heat of battle with the socialists and the Knights, and tempered by disillusionment with politics. Its designers had a far clearer perception of the Federation of Trades' shortcomings than they had of labor's plight in a mechanizing age. Its president, however, thought it (and himself) adequate to any challenge.

In December 1886, seated on his box-chair at his kitchen table-desk, Samuel Gompers set out to make the organized labor movement a growing, enduring reality in America. Eighteen years had passed since his first serious involvement — a time of painful lessons thoroughly learned. He had absorbed the wisdom of his mentors Strasser and Laurrell and left them behind as he pushed through the ranks to the head of the labor parade. Now that he was on top, he intended to stay there.

VI

Seven Fat Years and a Locust or Two

1886–1893

W HEN HE BEGAN work as president of the AF of L, Sam Gompers faced the challenge of his life. Would the federation succeed? Attempts to create a national labor organization had been made before, but all of them had failed. Gompers thought he knew why and believed he had learned from his own experience how to preserve the AF of L from a similar fate. He went to work confidently and aggressively to build an organization in his own image.

Building the AF of L required a mixture of offensive and defensive gambits. On offense the first task was always to recruit members. "Numbers," Gompers said, "give confidence not only to members but [also] to outsiders." But new recruits had to be consolidated systematically into disciplined units if the numbers were to be effective additions to the federation's strength. Gompers's earliest official efforts, therefore, "were concentrated in promoting stability of labor organizations" by inculcating the principles of business unionism in the affiliates. Business unionism, perfected by Gompers and Strasser in the cigarmakers' union, meant concentrating on shop issues — seeking higher wages and better working conditions; ignoring politics; providing a system of death, sickness, and unemployment benefits for members; exerting centralized control over strikes; and maintaining high dues. Above all, Gompers emphasized the importance of high dues: "Cheap unionism cannot maintain effective economic activity."

In the past, unions had grown during prosperity and withered during recessions. During the depression of 1873, for example, trade-union membership fell from three hundred thousand to fifty thousand. By combining recruitment with business unionism, Gompers hoped to end such oscillations. During good times, unions should grow as always. When hard times came they should retrench and accept any sacrifice necessary to hold onto members so that when prosperity returned they could march on undiminished.

Gompers saw membership as a three-part problem. First, he must persuade existing national trade unions to affiliate with the AF of L. Second, he must bring unorganized workers together into shop, local, regional, and then statewide organizations of their craft. Third, when enough statewide organizations developed in a trade, he had to collect them into a national body, incorporate the national into the AF of L, then cement the whole structure to the international movement. Gompers likened the relationship of the AF of L and the trade unions to the one that existed between the federal government and the political subdivisions of the United States; unions affiliated with the AF of L were like states; nonaffiliates were like territories that had to be built into states and then brought into the federation. Unlike the federal government, however, the AF of L reserved few powers to itself; the "states" retained an almost total autonomy over their own affairs and could secede at any time.

Gompers poured out exhortation and information. He told workers to organize and explained how to do it. He bombarded the officers of existing unions with letters urging the merits of affiliation and of business unionism. He took to the road, riding immigrant trains and cabooses, covering twenty thousand to thirty thousand miles a year to bring the gospel to the hinterlands. In February 1888, eleven months after taking office, Gompers reported to the executive council (the federation's officers) that he had spoken in "Syracuse, Rochester, Buffalo, Boston, Albany, Troy, Cleveland, Columbus, Cincinnati, Indianapolis, Louisville, Evansville, Nashville, Connellsville, Peoria, St. Louis, Springfield, Kansas City, Ft. Scott, Denver, Lincoln, Omaha, Sioux City, Minneapolis, South Bend, St. Paul, Milwaukee, Chicago, Grand Rapids, Saginaw, Lansing, East Saginaw, and Detroit."

Fortunately, he had a long period of prosperity to work with, because business conditions remained generally good until 1893. At first his efforts produced only a trickle of inquiries. Gradually, his tireless spadework turned the trickle into a flood. By the mid-1890s virtually every national union except the railroad-operating brotherhoods had affiliated with the AF of L.

Gompers also succeeded in organizing new local and national unions, including the streetcar men, painters, musicians, and teamsters. To old and new alike he preached the doctrines of business unionism and carefully timed economic action. Although he could truthfully say in 1918 that in thirty years as president of the AF of L, "I have never ordered a strike; and I have never decreed a strike, and I have never had the power to call off a strike when it was once inaugurated," his advice carried great weight and often determined the action of the affiliates, particularly those new to the movement. *"Do not strike in haste and repent at your leisure,"* he urged one local. "Strengthen your position so that . . . you have a good chance of victory before you strike. . . . It may be galling to wait for victory, but defeat is worse." To another he wrote,

My province is to advise and not to dictate. Therefore I will give you . . . my best judgment based on extensive observations . . . and acquaint you with [my] conclusions. . . . Unless present appearances are very misleading, strikes . . . will not be successful for some time. . . . Bide your time. . . . Your time will come if you have the courage to wait. Lost strikes break up your organization faster than any other cause.

By heeding Gompers's suggestions the affiliates made slow but measurable progress. The carpenters, for example, secured the eight-hour day in 1889. Each success made organizing easier and gave added credibility to Gompers's advice.

Membership in affiliated unions grew steadily. By 1892 it reached two hundred fifty thousand. These accretions eased the federation's financial stress, which in the early days was severe. Revenues came from a tax of one-half cent per member per week, collected by the affiliates and forwarded to the executive council in New York. At first many affiliates paid late and some not at all. Often there was no money for ink, paper, or the president's salary. In 1887, a discouraged Gompers wrote that he might have to give up and return to his trade. "If the unions of the country don't want a federation, then they don't and that settles it. . . . With a large family depending on me for support I cannot give my entire time without recompense."

As more money flowed in, Gompers reinvested it in larger offices and expanded staff. In 1893 he got authorization for a project dear to his heart, a newspaper called the *American Federationist,* which he served as editor, reporter, columnist, and proofreader. The federation also doled out money to support organizing drives and strikes. Although the affiliates consistently refused to authorize a permanent tax to build up a central strike fund, they did agree in 1889 to let the executive council levy a special assessment of two cents per member for five consecutive weeks. The special tax could be invoked only for a specific purpose, usually to aid a union on strike. Gompers noted that the reluctance of member unions to authorize a central fund stemmed from a lack of class consciousness ("The identity of interests of the toiling masses of our country has not been sufficiently recognized") and from the traditional American reluctance to surrender independence to a central authority ("The unions are acting on the belief that each should help itself before attempting to aid the other").

Growth of revenues and membership brought problems. Demands for money always exceeded the supply. Gompers rationed the cash as best he could and met waspish replies to his refusals of aid with patience and with the suggestion that support for a central fund might obviate such denials in the future. Financial problems within the affiliates added to Gompers's burdens. In the local and national unions, the policy of high dues often put large sums in the hands of men unaccustomed to handling them. Gompers supplied advice on accounting to prevent embezzlement.

The problem of overlapping jurisdictions was as bedeviling as finances. The distinction between crafts was often blurred, and an increasing number of disputes broke out between unions as to who should organize a particular group of workers. Resolving such disagreements became an important and time-consuming function for Gompers. The first case presented to the AF of L arose in 1889 between the carpenters and the furniture workers. Each year the number of disputes increased. Gompers at first tried to persuade the disputants to settle their differences themselves, but this voluntary method often failed. In 1893 the annual convention authorized the executive council to settle jurisdictional disputes by arbitration, provided both parties agreed. Keeping jurisdictional lines untangled was a thankless, time-consuming chore, but it had to be done to keep membership drives rolling.

Gompers's offensive strategies succeeded. Membership rose, and the unions made tangible progress on the economic front. In 1886 the AF of L, as Gompers himself realized, was a paper organization, handicapped by public opinion in the aftermath of the Haymarket Riot. By 1893 it stood, a quarter of a million strong, at the head of the American labor movement. Gompers had risen out of a crowd of agitators to national prominence. By speaking moderately in public and by insisting on compliance with the law, he had created a reputation as a responsible spokesman for an organization that the public gradually accepted as more respectable than menacing.

Two significant failures flawed this genuine progress: the affiliates did little to bring blacks, women, or unskilled workers into the AF of L's fold; and they failed to develop industrial unions in situations where craft unions made no sense. In plants where machinery replaced skilled labor, craftsmen of the type organized by AF of L trade unions constituted only a small fraction of the labor force, and that fraction was subdivided into many trades. Only a union that represented all the workers in each plant, regardless of occupation, could hope to exert much leverage against management. Unhappily for the AF of L, most of the mass-production industries moved swiftly to create just such highly mechanized installations and to replace skilled workers with semiskilled or unskilled, including an ever-increasing number of blacks, women, and immigrants. As a result, racism, sexism, and the antiimmigrant mentality of the AF of L's leadership as well as the craft-union form of organization stood in the way of organizing the industrial labor force.

Gompers was a bigot. Dozens of statements in his correspondence and in the *American Federationist* expressed the opinion put bluntly in his autobiography. "Of course," he declared, "I never entertained the thought of anything approaching social equality [for blacks]." Since his whole plan of trade-union action contemplated the elevation of workers to social equality, his often repeated claim that he favored fair economic opportunity for blacks cannot be taken seriously.

On the other hand, he was realist enough to know that unorganized blacks were a constant threat to unionized whites. "It isn't a question of social . . . equality," he told one organizer. "It is one of absolute necessity. If we do not make friends of the colored men they will . . . be . . . our enemies, and they will be utilized . . . to frustrate our every effort for economic, social and political improvement." Black workers frequently served as a "convenient whip [used by] employers to cow the white men and to compel them to accept abject conditions of labor." Whether spurred by this practical consideration or by a residual socialist belief in the unity of interests of the toiling masses, Gompers did resist overt expressions of prejudice by affiliated unions. He refused to accept the machinists in 1888 and the blacksmiths in 1893 because they had Jim Crow clauses in their constitutions. He admitted them when the exclusion was removed, though he knew that the change was on paper only; in practice the unions remained rigidly segregated.

As a realist and a politician, Gompers gradually abandoned his militant stand for a more pragmatic one, separate locals for blacks and whites. "It is useless . . . simply trying to ram our heads through a stone wall," he conceded. "Recognizing the conditions which exist is the best way we can . . . ultimately bring about a unity of feeling and action among all toilers." Gompers advised one local that since prejudice existed "and . . . many white workmen will not belong to the same local . . . with black men, and will not meet with them as members of the same local . . . [you should] go to work gradually to accomplish the desired effect. . . . Have the Union of white men organize, and have the Union of colored men organize also, both unions to work in unison and harmony to accomplish the desired end." Given the autonomy of the individual unions, Gompers had to yield to their segregationist policies to remain president of the federation. Only a personal commitment to equality great enough to outweigh his ambition and his sense of mission could have dictated a different stand. Gompers had no such commitment. Consequently, the American Federation of Labor was born white and essentially stayed that way in his time.

Similar circumstances precluded the enrollment of women. Gompers advocated it; the trade unions refused; Gompers acquiesced. Unskilled workers met a like fate, but in their case the inherent bias of skilled workers against the untrained was buttressed by a hostility to immigrants that spread through the trade-union movement in the early 1890s. In 1891, Gompers told the federation that the immigrant situation was "appalling." Times had changed; the development of industry and the closing of the frontier created a native-labor surplus that made it impossible for America to serve as the dumping ground for Europe's excess population. Gompers particularly objected to the Chinese and to immigrants from eastern and southern Europe because they were ignorant, unskilled, and unassimilable. "Some way must be found to safeguard America," he declared.

The Chinese were already prohibited (since 1882), and Gompers wanted the restriction maintained. In 1893, he advocated a device to keep out southern Europeans: the exclusion of illiterates. These sentiments had the wholehearted support of his fellow trade unionists, most of whom were either British or German as well as literate. The AF of L felt so strongly about this issue that it campaigned for antiimmigration laws, one of the few departures from its nonpolitical policy before 1906. The AF of L inherited the biases previously expressed by the National Labor Union and the Knights of Labor. Under the federation's policy of autonomy, Gompers could do little to overcome the limitations such discriminatory attitudes imposed. Much of the work force was thereby excluded from membership. Women, for example, constituted 16 percent of the labor force in 1870, 19 percent in 1880, 18 percent in 1890, and 20 percent in 1900. Immigrants played an even more prominent role, particularly in America's industrial cities. Compared to London with its 98 percent British population in 1880, immigrants or their children made up 78 percent of the population in Saint Louis, 80 percent in Cleveland, 80 percent in New York, 84 percent in Detroit, 84 percent in Milwaukee, and 87 percent in Chicago. In 1887, one observer commented that "not every foreigner is a workingman, but in the cities, at least, it may almost be said that every workingman is a foreigner." By the 1890s, the fear among some union members that the continuing influx threatened their jobs was compounded by the fact that many newcomers were unskilled and came from the alien cultures of southern and eastern Europe.

Sexism, racism, and antiimmigrant attitudes thus wracked the American trade-union movement, generating centripetal forces that repeatedly nullified solidarity. Theoretically, class consciousness could have overwhelmed bigotry, but the very persistence of such biases among American workers shows what little part class feelings played in their outlook. Whatever Gompers might tell his followers about the practical necessity for surmounting barriers of race and sex, the rank and file preferred to maintain their social attitudes, even when it cost them dearly.

For the AF of L the consequences of intolerance proved devastating, because prejudice against blacks, women, foreigners, and unskilled workers of all kinds combined with the prevailing craft-union mentality to prevent a program of industrial unionism. To his dying day Gompers defended the craft organization as the logically and historically correct method. He warned of "the awful calamity which is inevitable if trade union lines are not recognized and enforced." Unwilling to abandon a once successful strategy despite its increasing obsolescence, he also echoed the sentiments of the hard core of trade-union leaders who formed his power base in the AF of L. Industrial unions not only would have threatened the dominance of the crafts in AF of L affairs but also would have involved the organization of thousands of people whom craft unions despised, for organizing industrial unions would have required enrolling blacks, women, foreigners, and the unskilled.

Consequently, the AF of L cut itself off from the overwhelming majority of the labor force. Even after the passage of New Deal laws eliminating many of the practical obstacles to industrial unions, the AF of L leaders refused to venture into uncharted waters and justified their conservatism with the same arguments Gompers had used fifty years earlier. Finally, in desperation, a group of younger men, led by John

L. Lewis of the United Mine Workers' union, revolted and formed the Congress of Industrial Organizations (CIO) in 1936. After a long and often violent struggle, the CIO succeeded in doing what the AF of L had always refused to do — organize the workers in basic industries of American manufacturing.

Even though Gompers's offensive strategy in the AF of L's formative years concentrated on the crafts, the question of industrial unions proved troublesome from the beginning. Mechanization often caused jurisdictional disputes by combining several once distinct operations into a single mechanical functon. The tradesmen whose jobs were eliminated quarreled over who should control the machine that supplanted them. Worse, Gompers observed, as the machine permitted "the division and sub-division of labor, . . . many workers who have been employed at skilled trades find themselves with their occupation gone. . . . Thus we see the artisan of yesterday the unskilled laborer of today."

Gompers's reluctance to regroup the workers according to industry hardened as a result of his experience with the brewery workers' and the coal miners' unions, both of them industrial unions. The United Brewery Workers, an old organization, had come into the AF of L as an industrial union. The United Mine Workers, founded in 1890 and kept alive by financial transfusions from the federation, became an industrial union because the isolation of mining communities made craft locals impossible.

The two industrial unions involved Gompers in endless jurisdictional wrangles. The teamsters' union, for example, wanted to organize beer and coal wagon drivers. The stationary engineers wanted to enroll the boilermen at breweries and mines; the brewers and miners wanted to retain these men themselves. Gompers managed to negotiate settlements for these disputes, but it seemed to him that industrial unions and craft unions were incompatible. They spent as much time and energy assaulting each other as they did on the principal task at hand. One or another should be eliminated, and natural bias caused him to favor trade unions. In addition, personal animosity played a part. The leaders of the brewers and miners harassed Gompers incessantly through the mail and at the annual conventions of the AF of L. The brewers' president, for example, demanded that he lead a class movement by endorsing independent politics. ("The trade union movement is the only class movement in the country or the world," Gompers retorted.) The president of the United Mine Workers, with strong socialist support, defeated him in the AF of L presidential election of 1894, the only time he lost the office.

All this reinforced Gompers's faith in craft organizations and made his declared intention of organizing the unskilled an exercise in metaphysics. The growth of trade unions contributed to Gompers's inflexibility, for the bigger they got, the more he felt a vested and personal interest in protecting them, as a father instinctively protects his children and defends his methods of raising them.

From the beginning of the AF of L, Gompers, the federation, its constituent unions, and the narrow economic strategies they practiced came under attack from within and without. As they grew more powerful, they drew heavier fire, and Gompers devoted more and more energy to defense. In the AF of L's first years, employers presented less of a threat than did the Knights of Labor from without and the socialists from within. Happily for Gompers and the AF of L, the Knights contributed to their own downfall. After the failure of negotiations between the two organizations in 1886, the Knights launched a membership drive, but it did them little good. Endless internal wranglings, wars with the AF of L, and repeated structural revisions interacted with each other detrimentally. In the end the Knights broke down, because the idealism of the leadership was at odds with reality and because in allying themselves with the Populist party, they strapped themselves to a cadaver.

As time passed, the trade-union elements of the Knights grew disenchanted and either drifted away or were expelled. The Knights' loss often proved the AF of L's gain, since the same reasons that drove trade unions away from the Knights drove them toward the federation. Gompers's aggressive recruiting soon drew them into the AF of L's fold by exploiting the trade unions' disenchantment with theory and theorists. Trade unionists in the past had lamented that the labor movement had "been diverted from its original purpose through the machinations of charlatans and designing tricksters," had urged "that no wire-pulling, scheming, demagogues, no empirical charlatans, no visionary firebrands or other humbugs . . . be permitted within [the labor movement's] folds," and had resolved that *Labor's educators must come from Labor's ranks.* Theorists, experimentalists, and demagogues who have gained what notoriety they possess by prating about laborers' wrongs" must be eliminated.

Memories often succumbed to wishful thinking, however, and many trade unionists submitted for a time to the Knights' arduous advances. The Knights had an impressive assortment of theorists, experimentalists, and empirical charlatans of their own, a crew reinforced by the alliance with the Populists, led by a chautauqua of "visionary firebrands," "humbugs," and "demagogues." Characters such as Mary Ellen Lease ("the Kansas Pythoness"), Sockless Jerry Simpson ("the Prairie Socrates"), Bloody Bridles Waite ("the Lincoln of the Rockies"), Ignatius Donnelly ("the Sage of Nininger"), Cyclone Davis, and Calamity Weller were especially prominent. The gaudy panoply of the Knights and the Populists proved too much for hard-nosed trade unionists. One of them, wearied by the internal convolutions of the order, exclaimed, "What fool is there who thinks that the shoemakers of this country can be successfully organized and united under the banner of the Knights of Labor?" By 1888 the AF of L seemed a haven of sanity and pragmatism to such disaffected unionists, and to the haven they came. In 1892, the Populist party's defeat in the national election further depleted the ranks, and the depression of 1893 finished the job. The disintegration of the Knights of Labor left the AF of L supreme among American labor organizations, a position it held for forty years.

Gompers's internal foes put up a stiffer fight than his external competitors. To keep the Federation out of partisan politics, he had to subdue the socialists and others who saw the AF of L as a base for working-class political maneuvers. The AF of L's constitution stipulated that no one could join unless he held a valid membership in a trade union. Not all socialists were workers, of course, and most workers weren't socialists, but a good many were both. Since socialists were often among the most active members of their unions, they rose to positions of power and appeared as delegates at the annual AF of L convention. With metronomic regularity they urged their programs on the convention, kicking off what Gompers belittled as "the annual Socialist talk-fest." By the time the AF of L was founded, Gompers had had a bellyful of socialist rule or ruin tactics. He intended to prevent them from practicing either in the federation, and he fought them at every turn.

The first open clash came in 1889, when the Central Labor Federation of New York City applied for an AF of L charter. Scanning the list of the CLF's constituent bodies, Gompers noticed that it included the New York section of the Socialist Labor Party. He promptly rejected the charter application. The next year, Lucian Sanial, a socialist who had never belonged to a trade or labor union, appeared at the AF of L convention and presented credentials as a delegate from the CLF. The credentials committee, packed as all AF of L committees were with Gompers's henchmen, rejected Sanial. Gompers explained his position:

If you are a Socialist, why I shake you by the hands. Do you hold any other opinions, are you an anarchist, a single-taxist, are you a greenback reformer? Do you hold any other social or political belief? I do not care, but I say if you want to be represented upon an equality with every other trade union in the American Federation of Labor, you must produce a card of membership in your trade union. The condition precedent, I hold, to representation in a trade union movement is good standing membership in a trade union.

Warming to the task he added:

I say to you, friends and delegates, that the man who would accuse me or charge me with being an anti-Socialist says what he don't know anything about, he does not know Sam Gompers. I say here broadly and openly that there is not a noble hope that a Socialist may have that I do not hold as my ideal. There is not an inspiring and ennobling end that they are striving for that my heart does not beat in response to. But our methods are different.

The last sentence summarized the creed that justified Gompers's hostility to socialists within the AF of L. The method was everything. "Inspiring and ennobling end[s]" were fine to contemplate but useless as a guide to immediate action. Someday socialists and trade unionists might meet on the happy shore of some workers' paradise, but they were going there by different routes, and Gompers intended to travel light, not to burden himself with ideological baggage.

He summed up his methodological credo in a statement that became the byword of the AF of L's friends and foes for many years to come. "Trade unions pure and simple are the natural organizations of the wage workers to secure their present and practical improvement and achieve their final emancipation." The convention's two thousand delegates voted three to one to exclude Sanial, despite his claim that the Socialist Labor Party was "owned and controlled by wage workers . . . who are in full sympathy with . . . all the economic principles [of the AF of L] and who use this so-called 'political party' exclusively for the advancement of those economic principles." In this sense, Sanial argued, the SLP differed from "the old plutocratic parties," which were "notoriously the political machines of the employing class, and . . . a part of the whole machinery through which they control, rob and oppress their wage workers."

By rejecting Sanial's argument, the convention upheld the principle of keeping nonworkers and representatives of political organizations out of the AF of L. Next Gompers had to beat back an effort to drag the AF of L into socialism. In 1893, Thomas Morgan, a Chicago socialist and member of the machinists' union, introduced an eleven-point political program and advocated its endorsement by the federation convention. The preamble to the program called for independent political action by the organization, asked that the program be submitted to the AF of L's constituent organizations for favorable consideration, and requested that delegates to the next year's convention (1894, a congressional election year) be instructed to vote according to the results of the unions' referenda.

As Gompers said, "With one exception the program was a summary of legislative measures in support of which the federation was on record." These included compulsory education, an eight-hour law, employers' liability for workers' injuries, municipal ownership of streetcar lines, gas and electric plants, and the nationalization of telegraphs, telephones, railroads, and mines. The one exception, however, was a dandy. It demanded "the collective ownership by the people of all means of production and distribution." In other words, an endorsement of socialism.

Gompers saw that the program enjoyed considerable support in the convention. He decided to meet it with finesse, not force. He managed to get the term "favorable" stricken by the narrow vote of 1,253 to 1,182 and survived an attempt by the outraged socialists to unseat him as president. Debate on the resolutions occupied much of the space in the *American Federationist* and other labor newspapers throughout the year and consumed energies that Gompers felt could have been better used otherwise. "I knew," he said, "that for a year the labor movement would be in ferment, considering . . . Plank Ten [the socialist resolution], not the question of twenty cents an hour more or a shorter workday, but Plank Ten. And it was so."

When the 1894 convention's debate on the political program began, Gompers and his lieutenants attacked on two fronts. First, they denounced the preamble's suggestion for independent political action. Such behavior was desirable, Gompers argued, but only in the sense that individual workmen should vote for their friends and against their enemies. For the federation to endorse candidates or parties would have results "too portentous to contemplate," including "shattered hopes and unions destroyed. . . . A national labor movement cannot and will not succeed upon the ruins of the trade unions." The convention majority agreed and threw out the offending preamble.

Gompers then attacked Plank Ten. He declared it "not only controversial, but decidedly theoretical." If adopted, it would discourage "many sterling national trade unions from joining [the] battle . . . to attain first things first." Strasser and other cronies then took up the cudgels and introduced a series of substitute resolutions so absurd that the convention rejected the whole program, then separately endorsed all planks but number ten. The net result of all these machinations was that the socialists' "radical" political program was reduced to a reaffirmation of commitment to legislation the federation had already endorsed. "The Socialists raged helplessly," Gompers gleefully recalled. Some left the federation in frustration and disgust; others remained, vowing revenge. Gompers, however, thought that a small price to pay to preserve the AF of L as an instrument of "pure and simple" trade unionism. The socialists renewed their effort to harness the federation to their program in successive years, but never again came so close to victory.

Gompers avoided another political quagmire, Populism. Within the AF of L, as among the Knights, a considerable sentiment for affiliation with the Populists existed. The Populists had a stirring rhetoric of their own, and orators to cry it abroad. In 1890, Mary Ellen Lease denounced "government of Wall Street, by Wall Street, and for Wall Street. The great common people of this country are slaves, and monopoly is the master. . . . Our laws are the output of a system which clothes rascals in robes and honesty in rags. . . . The people are at bay, let the bloodhounds of money . . . beware." Farmers, she cried, should "raise more hell and less corn."

Other Populists explicitly courted labor's support for their growing political alliance. At the Populist convention at Omaha in 1892, Ignatius Donnelly inveighed against the system in which

urban workmen are denied the right of organizing for self-protection; imported pauperized labor beats down their wages; a hireling standing army, unrecognized by our laws, is established to shoot them down, and they are rapidly degenerating into European conditions. The fruits of the toil of millions are boldly stolen to build up colossal fortunes for the few, unprecedented in the history of mankind.

Stirring stuff that. But Gompers received it with his customary cynicism. In the *American Federationist,* he reviewed the preceding sixteen years and argued that changes of the party in power had done nothing to better the workers' lot. He forecast more of the same no matter who won. "I venture to predict that, so far as the wage-workers are concerned, it will matter little if President Harrison or some other Republican . . . or any member of the Democratic party . . . should be elected." Consequently, he said, many workers had left both parties, a sign of "sturdier manhood and independence, and a promise to maintain the liberties that the people now enjoy."

The defectors might well vote for the Populists, Gompers admitted, but it would avail them little. "To support the People's Party under the belief that it is a *labor* party is to act under misapprehension. It is not and cannot . . . be a labor party, or even one in which the wage-workers will find their haven. . . . Composed . . . mainly of employing farmers whose interests diverged from the workers'," the People's party could not achieve "cooperation or amalgamation [with] wageworkers' organizations." Such a union was impossible, because it failed the ultimate test of validity: it was "unnatural." During the campaign, Gompers said, the AF of L would maintain "a masterly inactivity. When the blare of the trumpets has died away, and the 'spell-binders' have received their rewards, the American Federation of Labor will still be found plodding along, doing noble battle in the struggle for the uplifting of the toiling masses."

At the AF of L convention in 1892, Populist sentiment ran high, despite the party's recent defeat in the national election. The convention endorsed two of the Populist planks: initiative and referendum, and government ownership of the telegraph and telephone systems. It also instructed the executive council to carry out a campaign of education that would increase trade unions' political activities. Gompers dealt with these instructions just as he had in 1886, when the first convention had urged full support for Henry George's gubernatorial campaign. He ignored them.

Gompers always boasted of the totally democratic nature of the trade union, but like other master politicians, he knew how to twist the democratic process into a ratification of his own intentions. When the conventions passed programs he agreed with, he adopted them. When he disagreed, he invoked "masterly inactivity." Between conventions, the rank and file paid little attention to the doings of the AF of L. They left things in the hands of the president and of the executive council. When convention time rolled around, Gompers counted on his ability to explain his conduct satisfactorily. Privately he justified his behavior — as politicians have always done — on the grounds that he knew better than his constituents what was good for them. He once told a colleague, for example, that machinists could not vote intelligently because they worked so hard and became so weary.

In public, he took a different tack. When his plans worked,

he divided the credit between his own sage leadership and the wisdom of the workers expressed through democracy. When his maneuvers failed, he unloaded the blame elsewhere: on the socialists within or on the greedy capitalists and corrupt politicians without. As the self-appointed personification of the trade-union movement, Sam rarely admitted to mistakes. But claiming credit and ducking blame was just one of the ploys by which Gompers consolidated his power. Although the president's term of office lasted only a year, Sam's adroitness as politician turned the annual elections into formalities. Only in 1894 was he defeated.

Gompers's hold on the presidency rested on his ability to build a dependable following. He did so with the skill and tactics of a political boss. Although the presidency theoretically bestowed little authority and prohibited interference in the internal affairs of the affiliates, the growth of the federation and of Gompers's own influence provided him with increasing quantities of that basic stock in the politician's trade, patronage. Gompers rewarded his friends by appointing them to committees, a perquisite that usually involved travel on the expense account. As national unions created paid offices, Sam's influence often helped his friends get elected to them. Sometimes he could wangle a trip abroad for one of his allies by appointing him fraternal delegate to an international labor conference. When a colleague lost his union job in some internal reshuffling, Gompers could sometimes secure him an appointment in the Bureau of Immigration or some other government department.

Gompers also had the power of the federation's purse at his disposal. By deciding on a union's application for financial aid in an organizing drive, Gompers and the executive council could exercise the power of life or death over a fledgling organization. The federation's relative poverty, especially in its first years, enhanced rather than detracted from this power, for when money was scarce, each dollar bought more.

Gompers used two other privileges of his office to advantage.

By traveling on the AF of L's business, he built a national following at the federation's expense. The *American Federationist* gave him a forum in which he could express his own opinions and shape the news to suit his own purposes. For example, he once urged an organizer writing a report of the typographers' convention to emphasize "those things which are commendable . . . and try to cover up those which will have a tendency to discourage or mislead."

Gompers combined these methods to build a core of loyal supporters, who annually reelected him and ratified his personal policies into federation principles. His allies led many of the largest national trade unions, and several were of British origin. Men like P. J. McGuire of the carpenters' union, G. W. Perkins of the cigarmakers', Tom Tracy of the typographers', James Duncan of the granite cutters', and Hugh McGregor of the seamen's union had backgrounds predisposing them to the trade-union structure that Gompers had observed during his youth in London. His principal opponents usually came from unions like the brewers', dominated by European socialists.

At the same time that Gompers consolidated his power within the union, he labored to improve the federation's national image. Although his followers sometimes engaged in violence, particularly against scabs and the Pinkertons who protected them, Gompers repeatedly denounced such behavior. He emphasized to newspapers, congressional committees, and the courts his opposition to lawlessness in any form. Speaking of himself, he said on one occasion: "I [have never] violated any law of the country . . . in which I live. I would not consciously violate a law now or at any time during my whole life." Of the movement he led, he declared: "Our publicly avowed . . . purpose has ever been to uphold and strengthen lawful and constitutional authority, to protect it against any invasion. . . . We would make the law supreme." American workers, Gompers argued, could "claim to be as patriotic and law-abiding as any other class of citizens" and could substantiate that claim by past actions "in times of public need and public peril."

As he became recognized as a responsible spokesman for the labor movement, Gompers received many invitations to testify before congressional committees and to confer with presidents on labor affairs. On such occasions Gompers took care to present himself and his organization as paragons of moderation. He emphasized the AF of L's commitment to American ideals and its willingness to work within the system. "The trade union movement," he declared, "is one of reason, one of deliberation, and depending entirely upon the voluntary . . . action of its members. It is democratic in principle and action, [and] conservative in its demands." He denied hostility to the American free-enterprise system, telling a congressional committee that it was "the best yet devised." By hewing carefully to this line, Gompers tried to dispel the menacing shadow cast by violent confrontations that periodically erupted between labor and its opponents. To Gompers, building an image was as essential as building an organization; neither was much use without the other.

As part of his image-building, Gompers avoided lost causes. After the Haymarket affair in 1886, he declined to participate in protests until 1887, when he endorsed a plea for clemency for the convicted anarchists. He carefully did so on the grounds that the trial had been unfair and on the humanitarian basis of opposing capital punishment. All the while he made clear that he had no sympathy with anarchism as a philosophy or with bomb-throwing as a strategy. He was determined to gain the American middle class's acceptance of the AF of L as a respectable, responsible organization by convincing the public that labor's goals were the same as everyone else's, and that labor intended to work within the system.

By 1893, when the depression came, Gompers had used his first seven years to good advantage. His offensive had built the federation into the nation's largest labor organization and had defeated the principal opponent, the Knights of Labor. His defensive skills had consolidated the gains by putting the unions on a business basis and had safeguarded those gains by keeping clear of politics. With the coming of the depression, he faced the first test of his plan to hold fast during hard times.

VII

Bad Business and a Bickering Crew Slow Up the Union Express
1893–1901

THE COUNTRY'S SECOND post–Civil War depression, which lasted from 1893 until the summer of 1896, proved the AF of L's ability to weather hard times. With the return of prosperity, the organization resumed the offensive, enrolling thousands of new members and pressing employers for better wages and working conditions. Businessmen, anxious to produce at full tilt now that the "Great Barbecue" had revived, often yielded to the pressure. Compared to the labor force, union labor steadily increased its wages and leisure time.

These successes vindicated business unionism and made Gompers, its chief architect, the foremost spokesman of organized labor in America. Encouraged by the federation's progress in the skilled trades, Gompers urged the affiliates to push forward with his plan to organize the unskilled as well, but the drive bogged down. As Gompers's hold on the organization tightened, he prosecuted his campaign against the socialists with mounting intensity, determined to protect the AF of L against those who might destroy it and to fortify his own position against those who might usurp it.

The depression of 1893 hit America hard. Factories closed; fifteen thousand businesses failed. Among the worst hit were many railroads. Overbuilt and overcapitalized, plundered by promoters like Jay Gould, one railroad after another slipped into bankruptcy. Sixty percent of them stopped paying dividends by 1894. Railroads had bulwarked the American economy for almost fifty years. Their financial needs had created the national capital market and the investment banking and stockbrokerage houses that serviced them. Their profits had sustained the confidence that made it possible for industrialists to use the resources of others to finance their own dreams of expansion. By 1890, the New York Stock Exchange, which had previously dealt almost exclusively in railroad shares, traded significant numbers of stocks and bonds issued to finance manufacturing ventures. Railroad bankruptcies and suspension of dividends scared off would-be investors just as railroad profits had enticed them; the flow of investment dried up temporarily, adding to the atmosphere of discouragement that is the prime mover in all depressions.

The railroads also contributed massively to the economy as employers and as customers. When the depression came, many railroads laid off workers and cut the wages of those who remained. They curtailed construction of new equipment and repair of old. When they stopped buying, many American firms lost their best customers, closed their doors, and sent workers home. The weakness of the railroads dealt a shattering economic and psychological blow to the whole society. The number of unemployed rose to four or five million, with millions more working reduced hours for short wages.

This second industrial depression in twenty years cast serious doubt on the American business system. When it worked, its abuses could be excused on the grounds that in time it would produce wealth enough to eradicate poverty;

when it broke down, these golden dreams became a nightmare of endless days spent looking for work where none was to be found. Workers saw their savings dwindle and their mortgages foreclosed. Neither unemployment compensation nor public welfare existed to mitigate the misery. The unemployed could fall back only on their own resources, on aid from charity, or on benefits from their unions. To critics it therefore seemed that the American version of capitalism could not provide steady work at decent wages and that the government could not or would not take up the slack in times of need.

Across the spectrum of American society and institutions came cries for change. Socialists demanded elimination of capitalism, Populists trumpeted the failure of the old political parties, Greenbackers and free-silverites peddled their monetary magic. In the economy, the decline in business weeded out the weak and encouraged the strong to combine, and a wave of mergers swept through American industry. Proud old family firms disappeared into the corporate anonymity of trusts and combinations, casting doubt on the ability of individual enterprise to survive.

Gompers had no such doubts about the AF of L. When the winds turned foul, he calmly steered the federation off its expansion course and rode out the storm. He retained his Marxist conviction in the permanence of industrialization. No depression could halt that process. In fact, the emergence of large firms amid the wreckage of small ones simply bore out another of Marx's predictions. Trusts did not worry Sam. He did not think their opposition to labor would prove as virulent as that of petit bourgeois capitalists (an expectation borne out by events in the long run). Moreover, as more efficient instruments of production, trusts promised to generate more wealth, which labor could share.

Gompers had boundless faith in America. His patriotism expressed itself in his belief that the American system of democracy and free enterprise permitted progress. His vision of America as a self-correcting mechanism bore a strong

resemblance to that of industrialists like Carnegie and Rockefeller, however much they differed on the ultimate outcome of
the process. In the 1890s Gompers opposed government intru-
sions into the economy as vigorously as any capitalist. He
thought legislation such as the Sherman Antitrust Act of 1890
would harm everyone. Such a law could only impede the
natural evolution of business, with the undesirable consequences that always attended interference in evolutionary
processes. "I have persistently held," he said, "that economic
organizations ought to be free to operate as economic needs
developed and that opportunity for initiative is essential to
sustained progress. This was why I did not join the hue and
cry against industrial combinations." In addition, Sam feared
that such weapons as the Sherman Act were as likely to be
turned on labor as on capital, another expectation later fulfilled.

His passion for America as a symbol sustained his views on
specific issues. "America is not merely a land," he declared. "It
is not merely a country, nor is it merely a sentiment. America
is a symbol; it is an ideal. The hope of all the world can be
expressed in the ideal — America." Upholding the ideal was
the duty of union men like everyone else. At the end of his life
he said, "A union man carrying a card cannot be a good
citizen unless he upholds American institutions." He had no
patience with reformers who attacked the country from
within. America shaped the union movement; the unions sustained America, and so it should be.

We American trade unionists want to work out our problems in the
spirit of true Americanism — a spirit that embodies our broadest
and our highest ideals. . . . We [built] the AF of L in conformity
with . . . the original intent and purpose of America. . . . With its
success are involved the progress and the welfare of the great mass
of American citizenship.

In these sentiments Gompers was much more in harmony
with his constituents than were the bombastic reformers who

peppered the air with inflammatory rhetoric. Populists like Ignatius Donnelly and fire-eating socialists like Daniel DeLeon might decry "robbing capitalists" and "corrupt political brigands"; pundits and philosophers might predict decline and doom for the bankrupt American system of business and politics; calls for revolution could echo on all sides; but no revolution came, either political or economic. Faith in America ran deeper than despair, and Gompers, sharing the faith, saw the depression as a temporary reverse, which, "upon the first revival of industry," would be followed by an upsurge in "our movement unparalleled in the history of America."

Gompers trusted in the trade unions' ability to survive the slump. He repeatedly urged caution: "Hold on to your organization by all means," he advised his affiliates. By and large they did. Unlike the depression of 1873, which nearly annihilated organized labor, the AF of L had nearly as many members when recovery came in 1896 as it had when the slump began. In 1897 it had 264,000 members, and Gompers could well declare himself "elated by the manner [in] which we have withstood [the depression's] fearful effects."

Survival of his organization massively reinforced Gompers's ego, for others had failed. The Populists fought national elections in 1892 and 1896, lost both, and evaporated as a party. The socialists divided into warring camps. The Knights of Labor expired. The AF of L endured, its structure intact. Confirmed in his wisdom by these events, Gompers resumed the organizational offensive in 1897, resisted criticism doggedly, and justified his defense of the status quo on the pragmatic ground that what worked was right.

As business recovered, the AF of L expanded rapidly, spending much of its income on membership drives. In 1894, its organizing budget was only $450. In 1898 it spent $1,300; in 1899, $6,400; in 1900, $16,000; in 1901, $32,000; and so on until 1904, when it paid out $83,000. In some years the federation spent a third of its total income on recruiting. From 1899 on it kept full-time organizers in the field. The effort paid off.

Membership rose from 264,000 in 1897 to 548,000 in 1900, to 1.7 million in 1904. In 1899, 9 international and 405 local and federal unions were added; in 1900, 14 international and 734 local and federal unions joined the federation's ranks.

Organizing was hard, often dangerous work. It demanded ceaseless travel and considerable courage, since organizers often met indifference or hostility among workers and violence from employers. Organizers were mobbed, beaten, shot at, and run out of town, particularly in regions like the coalfields, where the companies controlled jobs, housing, credit, local government, and the press. Persevering in the face of such opposition demanded a degree of loyalty and dedication no money could buy. Many of the most successful organizers, particularly in the brewers' and miners' unions, were confirmed socialists, sustained in their trials by the conviction that they were engaged in a crusade to develop class consciousness. Paradoxically, much of the growth in membership of which Gompers was so proud resulted from the work of men whose philosophy he despised. The antagonists coexisted successfully because they believed in the same means to different ends, and both awaited the outcome with confidence that their own vision would prevail. Gompers tolerated socialist organizers among the rank and file at the same time that he battled to keep them out of the leadership, because he believed he could lead the new members according to his own plan, regardless of what philosophy inspired them to join. The socialists labored on, following their philosophy of "boring from within" and believing that in time the converts would wrench the leadership from Gompers's conservative hands.

The partnership produced statistically impressive results — a sixfold increase in membership in seven years. The numbers, however, masked the federation's failure to make progress in organizing industrial unions. The implications of this failure in terms of potential membership emerged clearly in the light of one of the federation's few successful industrial unions, the United Mine Workers. In 1904, when the federation had 1.7 million members and dozens of trade unions affiliated, the United Mine Workers alone contributed 200,000 members to the total. Had other basic industries such as steel been similarly organized, the federation would have been enormously larger than it was. Nothing of the sort occurred; basic industries remained unorganized. The AF of L's drive peaked in 1904; membership remained stagnant thereafter until the First World War.

Two facts prevented the postdepression organizing drive from penetrating the ranks of industrial labor: the federation's internal weakness and the hostility of corporate management. During his years in the cigarmakers' union and in the nascent AF of L, Gompers consistently advocated the organization of both skilled and unskilled workers. Craft unions, he believed, could do the job. He saw no reason why the typographers, for example, could not enroll all of the employees in a printing shop, regardless of skill. As craft unions grew stronger, he confidently assumed that they would follow such a course. Unhappily, his hopes foundered on unexpected reefs. Many of the unskilled were reluctant to join unions. Easily replaced and unacquainted with the craft traditions that bound skilled workers together, the untrained laborers needed leadership and persuasion to overcome their reluctance. The craft unions, however, proved consistently unwilling to provide the necessary motivation.

Gompers's pleas for labor unity fell on ears stopped by the trade unionists' fear that the unskilled would dilute the movement's strength and by the traditional prejudices of white, male, skilled, northern European craftsmen. "The effort of organized labor is to protect and advance the interests of every wage earner, and to secure justice for all," he declared. "And experience has demonstrated that these can be best attained by a . . . comprehensive organization of the workers of all branches, in any given industry, under one jurisdiction." His argument, however, availed little. Much of the trade-union leadership shared Strasser's view of the unskilled as "tenement-

house scum" or worse. In his own union, Gompers had prevailed, but as president of the AF of L, with its constitutional
recognition of craft-union autonomy, he could not force his
colleagues to set aside their biases. In 1899, for example, the
tinplate workers told Gompers they did not want unskilled
workers in their union. Most shops, therefore, remained
divided between the organized craft workers and all others.

As business accelerated after the depression and the factory
system proliferated, the nature of the industrial work force
created a more formidable obstacle to craft-union organization
of unskilled labor. Many of the lines became blurred; more
often the majority of the work force consisted of large numbers of laborers whose occupation qualified them for membership in no particular union, or worse, in any one of several. In
small shops engaged in printing, or in the manufacture of
cigars, there was only one craft union on the ground, so no
jurisdictional problem existed. In large factories, however,
several different crafts were usually represented. A steel mill,
for example, employed puddlers, rollers, teamsters, boiler
tenders, plumbers, carpenters, and others, all belonging to
their craft union. The common labor was assigned as needed,
working with first one group and then another, or with several
at once. Which craft union should organize them, assuming
any of them had the will?

Gompers was unwilling and unable to interfere with the
affiliates' internal affairs. In the late 1880s he urged the creation of "industrial departments" in such industries as the
metal trades. Within such departments, he hoped, the craft
unions would decide among themselves who had jurisdiction
over unskilled workers and then set out to organize them. His
proposal was rejected repeatedly until 1907, and even after
that the departments spent most of their energies refereeing
jurisdictional disputes among skilled trades and accomplished
little among the unskilled.

The attitude of corporate management also hindered the
enlistment of the unskilled in trade organizations. The suc-

cessful creation of industrial unions in the brewing and mining industries resulted from an unusual combination of determined, broad-minded labor leadership on the one hand and the decentralized, proprietor-dominated industry on the other. In industries like steel, where the corporately owned, bureaucratically managed firm emerged as the dominant force in the 1890s, the craft unions found themselves under attacks that threatened to eliminate them altogether. They soon had more than they could do to preserve themselves as the agency of the skilled workers. To expand by absorbing the unskilled was out of the question. By 1900, Gompers had sensed the futility of trying to sell his craft-union supporters on a policy of organizing unskilled workers. If the affiliates wanted industrial unions, they had the means to build them any time they pleased. Since they clearly did not, he could only acquiesce. The AF of L convention in 1900 approved the continuation of the brewers' and miners' as industrial unions. Gompers, in a gesture designed to curry favor with craft unionists who wanted to break up the two industrial unions and redistribute their members into appropriate trade organizations, voted against the resolution.

The following year, the federation issued the "Scranton Declaration," which was authored by Gompers and which reaffirmed the principle of craft-union autonomy and declared that the AF of L should not adopt policies offensive to established trade unions. Together these added up to abandonment of efforts to force the industrial-union bone down craft-union throats and a recognition of the stubborn individualism of the rank and file who refused to surrender self-determination to central direction. In successive years, the socialists introduced resolutions favoring the creation of industrial unions, but Gompers and his supporters beat them back as often as they appeared. Since the federation had no way to coerce its affiliates, and since the executive offices of the AF of L remained largely in the hands of cigarmakers, tailors, granite cutters, and other craftsmen who jealously guarded their positions of authority by perpetuating their own narrow philosophy, neither the constituent unions nor the federation made a sustained effort to organize the new mass-production industries. Sporadic attempts by individual unions rarely succeeded. The Amalgamated Association of Iron and Steel Workers, for example, struck Carnegie Steel in 1892 and United States Steel in 1901. Both strikes failed, a cumulative catastrophe that destroyed the Amalgamated as a force in the steel industry and thereby eliminated the most promising base for organizing all workers in the country's most basic industry.

The Amalgamated itself was by no means an industrial union. Begun in the pre–Civil War era when iron was a craft industry, it was composed largely of English, Irish, and Welsh, who dominated the skilled trades in the steel mills. The Amalgamated had refused several times to organize the unskilled workers, who constituted an increasingly large segment of the steel-industry labor force as production became mechanized. Most of the common laborers came from the ranks of recent immigrants from southern and eastern Europe. Their presence ignited the traditional hostility of their elitist, British co-workers, a sentiment far stronger than class solidarity. Indeed, the skilled workers viewed the new arrivals not as potential allies, but as threats to their very existence. The failure of the strikes, nevertheless, dealt a blow to potential industrial unionization because the Amalgamated struck primarily for the right to act as bargaining agent for its members.

The strike against Carnegie Steel at Homestead in 1892 held particularly menacing implications for organized labor. It showed how easily one of the new giant manufacturing firms could crush a trade union if it chose, even an old, established one like the Amalgamated. It also showed that the management of such firms operated under pressures that made just such a hostile attitude likely. As long as Andrew Carnegie personally managed his firms, the Amalgamated survived and prospered along with Carnegie Steel. Carnegie remained essentially a proprietor in outlook, no matter how large his business. He boasted that he knew hundreds of workers on a first-name basis and that they addressed him the same way. On one occasion, just before speaking to an angry group of strikers, he told his fearful partners, "There can never be any hopeless troubles . . . as long as they call me 'Andy.' "

Carnegie's greed and shrewd business methods were further tempered in labor matters by a conscience nurtured in his boyhood among a radical Scottish working-class family. All these qualities, coupled to a flair for controversy and a perverse delight in twisting the tails of his fellow industrialists, prompted Carnegie to publish two articles in *Forum* magazine in 1886. In these articles he defended the right of workers to organize unions as "no less sacred than the right of the manufacturer to enter into associations with his fellows." He urged employers to recognize unions and bargain with them; he deplored the use of strikebreakers.

By and large, Carnegie practiced what he preached, encouraged by his general manager, Bill Jones, whose creed was: "Low wages [do] not always imply cheap labor. Good wages and good workmen [make] cheap labor." When Carnegie purchased the Homestead mills in 1889, he routinely renewed the Amalgamated's contract for three years. When renewal time rolled around in 1892, the union opened negotiations oozing misplaced confidence. The steel business was booming, they knew, so the company would hardly welcome a strike. Besides, "Andy" would look out for them.

Unhappily, a great deal had changed in three years. Bill Jones, the mediator, was dead. Carnegie, the prioprietor, was in Scotland. In the saddle at Homestead was Henry Clay Frick, facing his first major confrontation with labor since Carnegie, newly married and pondering retirement, had made him chairman in 1889.

The Amalgamated could hardly have faced a tougher antagonist. Not only did Frick have a vicious antilabor record running his own coke company, but in agreeing to the absorption of his company by Carnegie's, he had traded the certain authority of proprietorship for the subservient role of the hired manager. His personality did not bear the transition gracefully; he felt continually driven to prove himself to Carnegie, notoriously a hard master. Added to these burdens was a more compelling one that Frick shared with the new breed of hired managers throughout American industry, an obsession with costs.

Most nineteenth-century industrialists had a lopsided understanding of the workings of the market. The supply side they comprehended reasonably well; the demand side remained a mystery. That the market fluctuated erratically they knew from bitter experience. They had tried to control the oscillations and failed. Carnegie's answer and one widely copied, was simple. If the market could neither be controlled nor predicted, it must be dealt with by cutting prices until demand revived. The trick to surviving a depressed market, then, was to control costs to make a profit at the requisite low price. Some costs could not be reduced. Foremost among these was the interest due on borrowed capital. Indeed, the need for revenues to keep interest payments current exerted heavy pressure on managers to keep operating at a profit regardless of economic conditions. Added to this pressure was the need to generate revenue to pay dividends to stockholders and to buy and repair equipment so as to remain competitive.

Managers, therefore, struggled constantly to beat down the costs they could control, among them wages. Whenever the economy declined and prices fell, wage cuts usually followed. Carnegie's contracts with the Amalgamated took care of this automatically by means of a sliding scale that tied wages to the market price of steel. In these agreements, however, wages could not be reduced below a specified minimum, no matter how low the price.

In 1892 Frick, with Carnegie's passive cooperation, decided to reduce the minimum and get rid of the union simultaneously. No personal considerations restrained Frick. A brutal advocate of the supremacy of property rights, he regarded Carnegie's radical conscience as a detestable weakness and felt no such pangs himself; furthermore, he knew no workers and did not want to. The society watering holes of New York were his milieu, not workers' saloons. Yet it was not simply an exercise of his elitist antiunion sentiments that drove him, but also a desire to get a firmer grip on the cost side of the business. He made the Amalgamated an offer he knew would be refused. The union struck; Frick, like International Harvester's management before him, announced he would reopen the plant with nonunion labor and called for a force of Pinkerton detectives to protect the property. When the Pinkertons arrived, a pitched battle broke out. Troops poured in to restore order. The union continued to strike, confident that Carnegie would intervene as he had done before. But this time Carnegie, for reasons of his own, let matters run their course, a decision he regretted the rest of his life. Just before his death, he wrote, "No pangs remain of any wound received in my business career save that of Homestead."

Carnegie's pangs furnished no succor to the trade-union movement. The Homestead strike was broken, and Frick's tactics were widely imitated by corporate managers, sometimes with similar bloody results. Gompers noted the transition and its implications: "With the passing of Carnegie's personal management [began] the policy of antagonism to trade unions followed by the Steel Corporation." Prior to that time "the relations of the steel . . . companies to the Amalgamated . . . had been fairly amicable. . . . Things had been marching ahead with pretty even progress." The defeat at Homestead diminished the likelihood of an AF of L offensive into the basic industries. Together with the depression of 1893 and the events at Pullman, Illinois, in 1894, Homestead shifted Gompers toward the defensive, bringing "the labor movement squarely against the problem of holding its lines," rather than extending them. United States Steel's defeat of the Amalgamated in 1901 reinforced his defensive attitude and further

convinced him of the futility of combating the new corporations with industrial unions.

Gompers and his cohorts contributed to the failure of both
Amalgamated strikes. Jealous of their power and fearful that
support would generate a backlash that would weaken the
whole AF of L, they declined to bring the federation's financial or sympathy-strike resources to bear on the issue. In
1892, Gompers went to Homestead, spoke to the workers, and
raised some money for the relief of the strikers and for the
legal defense of their leaders. These efforts, however, were
essentially personal; he carefully kept the federation clear of
entanglement. In 1901 Gompers's support was even more
cautious; in fact, he abetted the negotiations settling the strike
on terms that virtually constituted surrender to the steel trust
and death to the union.

Gompers's role in the two steel strikes reflected his increasingly defensive thinking. By 1901 he had abandoned his
earlier commitment to the organization of all workers and
would gamble little to expand the federation if a loss might
damage it as it stood. The result was that although the organization expanded in membership, its scope remained largely
confined to a sector of the United States economy that declined in importance. "With the development of a movement
goes the responsibility for defense against efforts to tear it
down," Gompers said, and as the movement grew, such attacks
mounted, intensifying his defensive outlook as well as forcing
him into an ever deeper alliance with the craft-union leaders
who formed his core of support. The more he needed them,
the less likely he was to counter their wishes, an attitude
documented by the Scranton Declaration. Moreover, the
internal opposition to his strategy — "Gompersism" as it came
to be called — most often came from socialists and Populists,
who advocated industrial unions and alliance with political
parties, both policies distasteful to Gompers. His tendency to
despise opponents for personal as well as political reasons
magnified his opposition to industrial unions and politics.
Emotionalism harnessed to logic often makes a righteous

combination, particularly in defense of an ego easily bruised. In Gompers's case the mixture transformed the bold, venturesome, aggressive unionist of the 1870s and 1880s into the bickering, querulous, defensive labor boss of the 1890s.

Gompers's mistrust of the socialists and their programs waxed more intense than ever after 1893. "Socialists who believed in social revolution . . . and were too class-conscious to sanction a mutual agreement between employers and employees . . . were the most constant opponents of constructive policies," he observed. Stinging personal affronts reinforced theoretical differences. At the AF of L convention in 1894, the socialists, seething over the defeat of their cherished political program the year before, allied themselves with delegates disenchanted with Gompers's inaction during the Homestead and the Pullman strikes and defeated him for the presidency. John McBride, president of the United Mine Workers, took over and moved the federation's headquarters to Indianapolis. During his "sabbatical year," Gompers went to England as a fraternal delegate to the British Trade Union Congress, visited trade-union centers in France, Germany, and Italy, worked as an organizer for the United Garment Workers, gave lectures, and lobbied hard for relection.

Although Sam often declared that he never solicited votes, trusting in the wisdom of the members to make the right choice, in 1895 at least he was not adverse to nudging that wisdom in his own direction. He wrote George Perkins of the cigarmakers' union, who was lining up votes for him:

I am frank to say . . . that I would esteem it a pleasure to be again president of the Federation. . . . The movement . . . has become part of my very self, my yearnings, hopes — everything. . . . If you can show . . . a number of delegates that in the interest of our cause they ought to vote for me I am sure that you will do so and I shall appreciate your action beyond measure.

The effort succeeded. The 1895 convention in Denver reelected him by the narrowest margin in the history of the federation, 1,041 to 1,023. Gompers never lost again. The socialists, who had united their factions briefly in 1894–1895, fell back in disarray before the counterattacking Gompers machine. The more conservative socialists determined to remain within the federation and cooperate with Gompers while building strength for fresh attacks. It was among this group that the federation found many of its most effective organizers for its post-1893 membership drive. Although their dreams of taking control of the federation never came true, the conservative socialists remained a force in the AF of L; together with their communist cohorts, they dominated the leadership of some of its affiliates and played a major role in organizing CIO industrial unions in the 1930s. Their radical energies thus provided some of the driving force in creating America's two most successful labor organizations, though the organizations themselves remained staunchly conservative.

The more radical element set up a dual organization — the Socialist Trade and Labor Alliance, an arm of the Socialist Labor Party led by Daniel De Leon. A figure more certain to fire Gompers's rage could scarcely have been imagined. De Leon was not a worker and never had been. Worse, he had been a professor at Columbia University and thus epitomized the very type of intellectual, dabbling in labor affairs, that Gompers had despised since boyhood. De Leon was a doctrinaire socialist of ideology so pure that Lenin eulogized him as a pioneer in world socialism. Finally, De Leon had an acid tongue, which he turned on the AF of L generally and on its leader specifically. The AF of L, De Leon said in 1896, was a "tapeworm," led by "ignoramuses" and "Labor Fakirs" who browbeat the membership out of their dues so that "they may attend the annual rowdidow called the 'A.F. of L. Convention.'" In the hands of these "misleaders," De Leon scoffed, the federation "ship, never seaworthy," had become "stranded and captured by a handful of pirates"; it was "a tapeworm pulled to pieces."

This attack roused Gompers's belligerent instincts at once. He denounced the Socialist Trade and Labor Alliance as just one more dual union. "The work of union smashing," he observed in the *American Federationist,* has "been taken up by a wing of the so-called Socialist Party of New York headed by a professor without a professorship, a shyster lawyer without a brief, and a statistician who furnished figures to the Republican, Democratic, and Socialist Parties." These "mountebanks," Sam warned, had created "a brand new national organization with the avowed purpose of crushing every trade union in the country" and had "launched [it] from a beer saloon." (A beguiling touch from a man to whom the beer saloon was a second home.)

The billingsgate continued as the years passed. De Leon denounced Gompers "as an agent of the stock exchange, starting strikes to lower stock, or keeping up strikes to favor competing concerns." Gompers in turn described De Leon's newspaper, the *People,* as "that mudslinging machine of six thousand jackass power." His hostility to De Leon certainly pushed Sam into increasingly virulent opposition to socialists and contributed to his denunciation of them in 1903 as economically unsound, socially wrong, and industrially impossible. Doubtless he was right, for De Leon's brand of socialism drifted steadily away from the workers and became an arena for frustrated intellectuals and genteel reformers.

Gompers, on the other hand, understood and shared the views and aspirations of the workers and shaped the AF of L to reflect them. Like most American workers, he accepted capitalism as the engine that would keep progress in motion. Unlike his European counterparts, who moved increasingly to the socialist position that the state should own all means of production, Gompers came to accept private property. European labor leaders argued that workers should earn a living wage always; if this resulted in the bankruptcy of the firm, then society at large should make up the deficit, preferably by assuming ownership and continuing operations. Gompers, for his part, acknowledged the necessity of profit, declaring in 1883, "I believe that in modern society and so long as the competitive system lasts . . . the employer is entitled to a return . . . if he is willing to pay living wages." Firms that could not afford to pay living wages should be "crushed out" by more able, competitive companies, not taken over by government.

This logic led Gompers to accept giant corporations and trusts, despite their abuses and their hostility to unions, on the grounds that workers would ultimately benefit from their efficiency. His distrust of government and politics extended to his economic logic. Watching the corruption and inefficiency of the governments of Grant, Hayes, Garfield, and Arthur, Gompers saw small cause to believe that the workers could benefit from placing their economic fate in such tainted hands. Governments that could not handle the minimal business of collecting the tariff, of delivering the mail, and of managing the public lands and the national monetary system without perpetual deficits, bribery, and swindles could scarcely be entrusted with the management of the complex industrial system.

Capitalism thus resided in Gompers's breast as it did in the majority of his fellow workers. So it remained. In 1905 the European economist Werner Sombart observed the "intimate . . . relation of the American laborer to capitalism. . . . I believe he enters into it with all his heart: I believe he loves it. . . . The greater intensity of American labor is nothing more than the expression of the laborer's fundamentally capitalist mental attitude."

As Sombart's observation implied, the trade-union movement (which in 1904 reached an all-time-high membership) did little to achieve working-class consciousness. One leader commented in 1887 that "there is an instinctive feeling among trade unionists that when they form a union they do not surrender their individual politics or religion." Workers retained their sense of individuality, which they derived from sentiments that cut across the theoretical class lines, and declined to accept dictation from union leaders in such matters.

To some extent the workers' reluctance to accept class consciousness resulted from large numbers of them belonging to the Catholic church. Socialism was anathema to Catholicism, for socialist philosophy denounced religion as the opiate with which the bourgeois kept the masses in a state of drugged submission, argued the perfectibility of man and the redemption of society through an entirely secular process, and denied the fundamental Christian concepts of original sin and redemption by divine intervention. Hence Catholicism reinforced the prevailing antisocialist ethos in the United States and placed a stamp of religious approval on the worldly instincts that supported capitalism.

The very nature of American trade unions also reinforced the workers' capitalist outlook. Many unions forming the bedrock of the AF of L organized the workers in traditional trades that long predated industrialization. Gompers's own union was one such, and its strongest allies came from among the building trades, printers, cabinetmakers, tailors, coopers, and other ancient crafts. Such workers, as Gompers noted, rarely exhibited class consciousness; they shared a set of attitudes associated with a common work experience, attitudes at whose core burned a sense of independence born of the mastery of a valuable trade and often achieved through a long apprenticeship. These tradesmen did not see themselves as flotsam, washed about on the sea of industrial labor. They regarded themselves as entrepreneurs, whose stock-in-trade was their craft, which enabled them to move freely from place to place and from job to job. Often they went in business for themselves, but just as easily abandoned that role to resume working for someone else.

The trade union bolstered its members' sense of independence. It kept them informed of job openings across the country and supplied them with travel funds, just as the London cigarmakers' union had subsidized Solomon Gompers's crossing of the Atlantic. In any town where his union had a local, a tradesman could count on help finding work and on unemployment benefits if no jobs were available. In any shop run under union contract, the organization protected its members against capricious firing, unpaid overtime, and other employer abuses, leaving the members free to live and work as they liked as long as their work met agreed-upon standards.

Thus, as George Bernard Shaw observed, trade unions were not socialism, but the capitalism of the working class. As Gompers's distrust of politics and socialism hardened, his reliance on the trade union as the instrument of workers' improvement intensified. Under Gompers's firm guidance, the AF of L grew by appealing to the conservative, procapitalist sentiments of craft workers and their unions. In the process, organized labor emerged as one of the pillars supporting the American industrial establishment. Gompers often exhibited a debt to the socialist associations of his youth, including a willingness to use the language of class hostility when it suited him and a Marxist acceptance of the inevitability of industrialization. These characteristics, however, no longer reflected a doctrinaire outlook, for he left that behind as he matured. In its place he developed a commitment to the typically American traits of pragmatism and eclecticism. He used what worked, regardless of its source, but aligned himself with no movement save his own, which he kept attuned to the attitudes of his constituency. When a friend asked him to challenge the existing order by leading the workers into politics as an organized, revolutionary force, Gompers replied, "Would you have me lead them . . . where they have shown their unwillingness to go?"

By leading the workers shrewdly toward goals they believed in, using methods they endorsed, Gompers solidified his own position, strengthened the AF of L, and improved its members' status. These gains, however, resulted not only from Gompers's wisdom and the skill of the workers, but also from the preindustrial nature of the industries where most of them worked. In the older industries mechanization came slowly, attempts at merger frequently failed, and independent contractors as well as job shops remained the characteristic unit of production well into the twentieth century. Against such small employers, trade unions exerted considerable leverage, which often made it possible for them to tell employers whom to hire and to negotiate raised wages, shortened hours, and improved conditions.

In industries where the magic of chemistry, electricity, and the internal-combustion engine offered massive economies of scale through mechanization, the AF of L made little progress. In these fields large corporations thrived, minimized skilled labor, did their own hiring, arbitrarily determined conditions of employment, and fought unions vigorously. Gompers observed the devastating consequences of labor's encounters with these new goliaths, but retained his conviction that the trade unions could bring them to heel. It would take time, but he was patient. In the meantime, he felt greatly encouraged by progress already made.

The AF of L's ability to hold its own during the depression of 1893, together with its success in the boom that followed, confirmed to Gompers the unique strength of the craft union, the virtues of business unionism, and the wisdom of his own leadership. His determination to preserve them all underlay his reluctance to press for organization of the unskilled and his relentless opposition to the socialists. Despite occasional setbacks, he expected to lead the AF of L on to the ultimate goal — the organization of all workers, regardless of occupation or degree of skill. Meanwhile, he followed the practical course of placating his allies and harassing his enemies. Most important, perhaps, he labored to keep the federation free of political entanglements and strove to beat back an increasingly effective counterattack mounted in the courts by his opponents in business.

VIII

The Populists Go Under, Big Business Digs In, Small Business Goes to Court

1893–1906

THE POPULIST MOVEMENT generated excitement that lured many American unionists, not only in the Knights of Labor but in the AF of L as well. From the rank and file came demands for an alliance, which delegates brought to the floor of the AF of L's annual convention in the early 1890s. Mature, confident, sure of his course, and full of fight, Gompers resisted with guile, sarcasm, and parliamentary skill, then watched with satisfaction as the Populist ship sank in 1896 with the Knights of Labor, but not the AF of L, on board.

At the same time, a far more threatening menace than the Populists appeared to confront organized labor. Business, seeking a way to neutralize the AF of L, seized upon the Sherman Antitrust Act and found it a deadly weapon. Gompers met its thrust head-on in the courts and on picket lines but suffered a series of stinging defeats that threatened to nullify his past achievements and his future ambitions.

As the Populist party rebounded from its defeat in the presidential election of 1892, the pressure on Gompers mounted. Buoyed by success in western state elections, fired by the frustrations of the three-year-old depression, the Populists cast their lot with William Jennings Bryan, the Democratic presidential candidate in 1896. The Democratic-Populist platform consisted largely of planks that the AF of L had already endorsed as desirable legislative goals. This, however, did not sway Gompers from his stand of official neutrality by the AF of L. "I will endeavor to the very best of my ability to keep out of the maelstrom of party politics," he wrote. In pursuit of that aim, he sent a circular to the affiliates, warning them to be wary lest their spirits be stirred by "the partisan zealot, the political mountebank, . . . the effervescent, bucolic political party, [the] cure-all sophist and fakir." Labor organizations had followed such siren songs in the past, he added, and had followed them to destruction.

The circular touched off a hostile reaction among the craft unions, many of whom had endorsed Bryan or planned to do so. Fresh from his own narrow reelection the year before, Gompers tried to placate his angry followers by issuing a new circular, claiming he had been misunderstood. Whether "partisan zealot," "political mountebank," and "bucolic political party" fairly described Bryan and the movement he led, both went down to defeat, and Gompers rejoiced that the trade-union movement had "weathered the storm successfully." Bryan's defeat confirmed Gompers's faith in his own wisdom in refusing to endorse Bryan despite a deluge of letters and telegrams from constituents urging him to "get off the fence." Sam remained convinced that trade unionists should vote independently for candidates of their own choice and that the federation should restrict its official political efforts to lobbying for selected legislation.

Gompers's lobbying efforts straddled his views and the wishes of his constituency. Occasionally this placed him in an awkward position, saying one thing and doing another. In general, he followed his conscience and ignored federation resolutions that he personally disapproved. He rarely defied instructions openly; he simply bogged them down through inaction and blamed someone else for the lack of results. Gompers favored only those laws that might bring benefits that labor could not hope to achieve through direct bargaining with employers, even if such bargaining had never succeeded in the past. All other legislation he consistently opposed. Consequently, the AF of L endorsed various planks in the Populist program aimed at reforming the banking system, at securing government ownership of transportation and communication, and at similar measures to modify the national economy. The AF of L also advocated direct election of senators, use of the secret ballot, establishment of initiative, referendum, and recall, and limitation of immigration. All of these measures lay outside the domain of labor-management relations and could not be furthered by trade-union bargaining.

In the area of laws relating directly to labor, Gompers took a much narrower stand. Although the federation passed resolutions favoring universal eight-hour legislation, Gompers himself supported it only for government workers and for those engaged on federal government contracts. He made this exception because in such cases the government was the employer, and there was no way to bargain collectively with the national government. For a time in the 1890s he concurred in a federation mandate that favored maximum-hours laws for women but gradually abandoned even this modest stand.

In one significant area, employers' liability and workmen's compensation, Gompers differed irreconcilably from his rank-and-file members. In the late nineteenth and early twentieth centuries, employers were virtually immune from damage claims by injured workers or by the survivors of workers killed on the job. This meant constant, grinding hardship for many and for their families; it was more dangerous then to work in America's mines and mills than it was to fight in its wars. The United States had the highest rate of industrial accidents in the world: every year a half-million or so workers were injured, and some thirty thousand killed. More men died in coal mines than in all America's wars.

To a large extent this slaughter resulted from employers' disregard of safety. The courts held that employers were not liable for damages if the accident involved the worker's own "contributory negligence" or the negligence of a fellow employee, or if the worker could be expected to know the dangers and had therefore "assumed the risk" by taking the job. In such circumstances, employers felt little incentive to spend money to prevent accidents, and only a few of the more humane bothered. This was a burning issue to workers, and trade union affiliates hammered away at state legislatures for laws to make employers responsible. They also pressed the AF of L to lobby for similar laws in Washington. But Gompers declined to participate, except to urge such protection for federal employees.

Gompers also opposed the passage of old-age pensions, unemployment compensation, and compulsory health insurance, all measures dear to the heart of many of his followers. In 1907, the federation directed the executive council to work for a law providing pensions to employees of the federal government, but Gompers ignored the instructions. Only in the field of child-labor laws did Gompers consistently concur with his constituents and push for remedial legislation.

Gompers's opposition to legal remedy resulted from the fusion of two traits: one, his deep distrust of the political process, and two, his vanity, both of which led him to resist any tactics that might transfer labor's potential power from the trade unions, where he could direct it, to the political arena, where it was beyond his control. Childhood experiences convinced him and many of his fellow immigrants that politics was a game played by the elite to the detriment of the commonality. When trade unions involved themselves in party politics, they committed suicide, as in the case of the National Labor Union and the Knights of Labor; when they kept clear, they survived. Moreover, legislation provided labor with a weapon of dubious value. The Cigarmakers' drive for anti-tenement legislation had shown that vividly. After years of lobbying, which consumed time and money better used in organizing unions and strikes, the union succeeded in getting the law passed only to see it struck down by the courts. Even more, Gompers feared that laws that nominally protected labor could somehow be twisted by the courts into weapons useful to employers.

Thus Gompers justified opposition to maximum-hours and minimum-wage laws on the grounds that employers would then compel workers to work at those standards, preventing effective bargaining for higher wages or shorter hours. "When that times comes," he said, "when by statutory enactments wages are set, it will only be another step to force working men to work at the behest of their employers, or at the behest of the state, which will be equivalent to . . . slavery."

He explained his decision to withdraw support for maximum-hours laws for women by arguing that "this woman movement is a movement for liberty, freedom of action and thought," a movement leading to a time "when women shall be accorded equal independence and responsibility with men, equal freedom of work and self-expression." As part of this responsibility and independence, women would have to organize and improve their own lot in the workplace, rather than rely on the doubtful aid of government agencies. In this area, as in the field of eight-hour legislation, Gompers dragged his constituency around to his view. In 1915 the federation reversed its official position favoring eight-hour laws, and although it never officially retracted its support of the women's movement, such support remained nominal. Once the women's suffrage movement got under way, Gompers could justify his attitude on the grounds that with the vote women would enjoy an equal footing with men, should join trade unions, and go on from there.

Workmen's compensation laws, he argued, would result in

endless lawsuits between employers and employees, which workers could ill afford. Old-age pensions would serve as an excuse for employers to refuse to bargain on the subject with trade unions. Strong unions, Gompers claimed, could secure more effective retirement plans than would ever be enacted in law. Unemployment compensation was a "utopian dream." Better that the workers should spread the work by enforcing eight-hour-day clauses in their contracts and by refusing to work overtime. State health insurance he rejected as an unwarranted intrusion on the workers' rights and as an insult to their dignity in that it implied that the workers could not take care of themselves and that the state must therefore become their guardian. Such an idea, he said, was "repugnant to a free born citizen." Testifying against such legislation before a congressional committee, Gompers pulled out all stops. "As I live, upon the honor of a man . . . I would rather help . . . a revolution against compulsory insurance and regulation than submit." Although the sickness, injury, or death of his fellow workers made him "heart-sore, ill, and sad," he declared that "[he] would rather see . . . the illness, the killing and maiming . . . go on for years and years, minimized and mitigated by the organized labor movement, than give up one jot of the freedom of the workers to strive and struggle for their own emancipation through their own efforts."

Gompers exhibited a mixture of common sense, disingenuousness, cruelty, and selfishness. In some cases he was right. Unions, for example, often succeeded in negotiating better pensions than those provided by social security; liability suits involved a long, frustrating process. On the other hand, Gompers might not have contemplated "years and years" of "killing and maiming" with such equanimity had he observed it in a coal mine rather than from the safety of the federation's headquarters. Finally, union leaders historically guarded their power jealously and resisted policies, however beneficial, that might weaken the workers' reliance on their union and its leaders.

Whatever his reasons, they led him into a policy that had unfortunate consequences for the movement he headed. His opposition delayed the enactment of measures that, on the whole, proved beneficial. Furthermore, had he had his way and achieved his ends through bargaining alone, the benefits would have been restricted to members of AF of L unions, never more than a small minority of all American workers. The rest would have been left to fend for themselves. By rejecting the political process, moreover, Gompers shifted the trade-union movement away from the locus of power in American society and nullified much of its potential effectiveness. Labor could have exerted effective pressure, even under Gompers's doctrine of individual action by labor voters. Individual unions contributed to the passage of workmen's compensation laws at the state level, despite Gompers's personal opposition. The AF of L could have functioned similarly at the national level and added to its appeal to the workers, rather than diminishing it as Gompers feared.

His opponents, the employers, showed no hesitation in manipulating the political-legal process to their own ends. By attacking through the courts, they forced Gompers to enter politics in spite of his reluctance. When he did so, in 1906, it resulted not from a desire to carry the AF of L's offensive into wider fields, but from the overwhelming necessity to defend the trade union movement's legal rights to organize, bargain, and employ its traditional weapons of strikes and boycotts. By 1906 the AF of L was involved in a fight for its life, its very existence threatened by the courts' interpretations of the Sherman Antitrust Act of 1890.

The legal corpus consisted of two kinds of law, statute and common. The former embodied all specific measures, such as the Sherman Act; the latter was built up over the years by decisions made in contests where no specific law existed or where a law's constitutionality or applicability was disputed. Both protected society at large against its individual members, or members of society against each other. As referee, the courts balanced individual rights against the claims of the general welfare.

Statute law was presumably simpler than common law by virtue of its specificity. Common law was more complex because it was whatever judges said it was. Judges made common law on the basis of a theoretically rational but in fact highly subjective system of precedents and natural law, mixed judiciously with considerations of individual privilege and public welfare. Since all of these concepts were vague and ambiguous, especially in a complex society, their application to specific issues became largely a matter of individual interpretation. Common-law cases dragged the disputants into a legal thicket impenetrable to laymen. Guiding clients through this maze made the legal profession one of America's growth industries. Labor leaders, rarely lawyers themselves and possessed of scant means to employ expert counsel, always operated at a disadvantage in the legal jungle.

Unhappily, judicial neutrality was the exception rather than the rule. Most judges' backgrounds inclined toward property and capital. In addition, their interpretations could sometimes be influenced by bribery, nepotism, or the promise of higher appointment, inducements that labor could rarely proffer. The Sherman Act dragged the AF of L into a series of battles in which it found itself repeatedly worsted. The Sherman Act forbade conspiracy in restraint of trade; its justification was Congress's constitutional right to regulate interstate commerce. The act, which seemed simple enough at first glance, illustrated how unspecific a statute could be, for every word of its operative clause demanded interpretation. What constituted a conspiracy? Could a labor union be interpreted as one? What constituted restraint of trade — a strike? a boycott? What, in fact, was trade? For a time the Supreme Court held that manufacturing was not trade; hence, it was exempt from the Sherman Act.

For Gompers, the Sherman Act turned out to be a nightmare come true in the form of a law aimed at regulating capital but used to assault organized labor. He had distrusted the bill from the start: "Though I had been watching with keen apprehension the growth of industrial trusts," he said,

I followed the making of that law with a feeling of even greater disquietude. . . . Since in the legal vocabulary normal union activity and conspiracy were interchangeable terms, I was convinced that if trade unions were not specifically excluded from the provisions of the measure, the law would be applied to the organized efforts of the workers.

Gompers lobbied hard for such an exclusion but to no avail. Labor had long struggled in the state courts to win the legal right to organize and to use strikes and boycotts. Under the Sherman Act, the federal courts might interpret union organizations as conspiracies and union weapons as restraint of trade.

Organized labor had fought the conspiracy charge before Gompers was born. In 1842, Chief Justice Lemuel Shaw of the Massachusetts Supreme Court in *Commonwealth* v. *Hunt* held that unions were not conspiracies and that strikes were not illegal even if they intended to impoverish another — that is, to diminish his gains and profits. In succeeding years, unions kept up the battle to legitimize strikes and boycotts and gradually won the principle at the state level that such tactics were not illegal so long as they aimed at legitimate goals. These goals the courts generally defined as improvements in wages, hours, and working conditions.

Under the Sherman Act, Gompers feared all this might be lost. If business convinced the courts to apply its clauses to trade unions, then union activity could be prevented by the use of injunctions secured by employers from federal courts. An injunction, a court order prohibiting specific activities, subjected violators to fine or imprisonment for contempt of court. It was a civil remedy, designed to prevent acts that deprive another of his rights in a way not specifically proscribed by law or to prevent in advance unlawful acts that might cause damages that cannot be compensated for afterwards. Thus an employer could seek an injunction against union organization, against a strike, against a picket line, or against a boycott on grounds such as violation of contract or on the basis that a strike or boycott deprived the employer of the free use of his property and of the income he could derive from it. If, for example, an employer could convince a judge that strikers might run amok and burn down his factory, the judge would issue an injunction against union activity because, although arson was a criminal offense and the culprits presumably would get their just deserts, the employer would have no way of collecting damages from imprisoned vandals.

That judges had a right to issue injunctions to prevent arson, trespass, and sabotage, no one, not even Gompers, bothered to deny. On the other hand, strikes, picket lines, and boycotts presented no such immediate threats to property; rather, they threatened expectant gains by disrupting production and sales. In order to justify injunctions to protect "probable expectancies" and customer goodwill, two steps had to be taken. First, such "expectancies" had to be interpreted as property rights. But this alone would not serve, since courts had decided that no recovery could be made of losses resulting from the exercise of legitimate rights. The second step, therefore, was to have strikes, picketing, and boycotts declared illegal. State courts in general had refused to do either, but the passage of the Sherman Act opened the possibility that federal courts might agree to act where state courts had declined.

All this Gompers dreaded and he had not long to wait. Between 1890 and 1894, injunctions were issued in minor labor disputes on the grounds that a trade union conspired to restrict trade. These cases heightened Gompers's apprehensions for the future. Torn between his commitment to law on the one hand and his feeling that "government by injunction" was inherently undemocratic on the other, Gompers had a limited choice of options. Unions could go to court and contest the injunction before it was issued, or he could advise his followers to defy injunctions once they appeared. He himself had done so in the past and gotten away with it. Moreover, he felt that injunctions regulating industrial relations were illegal, so defying them did not contradict his belief that labor must stay within the law. "Many injunctions," he argued, "have sought to prohibit workers from exercising their constitutional rights. Such injunctions had no real authority" and ought to be resisted. "Resistance to tyranny is obedience to God," he declared, and he had no doubt that elimination (by injunctions or by any other means) of the right to strike invited tyranny. "Show me a country [where] there are no strikes," he said, "and I'll show you that country [where] there is no Liberty." Since the ultimate guardians of liberty were the people, Gompers thought it necessary to bring the issue of injunctions before the public, even if it meant going to jail. This method had its drawbacks. Not only might it remove labor leaders from the heat of the picket line to the cooler confines of a cell, but, in addition, civil suits against violators of injunctions often sought and won multiple damages for losses. A single adverse decision in a major case could bankrupt a trade union, or the AF of L itself.

Contesting and defying injunctions carried the trade-union movement beyond its own direct negotiating methods and into the arms of lawyers. Gompers had no more faith in this breed than had the Knights of Labor who had excluded attorneys on the grounds that they were parasites. Few could be counted upon to prosecute labor's case vigorously. Gompers well remembered that Strasser had paid Roscoe Conkling $1,000 of the Cigarmakers' scanty cash and gotten neither results nor a refund. Later experiences did little to change Gompers's mind:

It is a fact, that despite one invasion after another which the judiciary has made upon the rights of the citizens, we find few if any members of the . . . practising legal profession to challenge the jurisdiction of a court upon a fundamental constitutional law when the violation of rights affect workmen engaged in an industrial dispute with employers. The bench has moved forward, and practising attorneys have yielded ground and continuously conceded rights guaranteed by our constitution.

Despite his reservations about the legal profession, Gompers until 1894 generally fought injunctions before they were issued or defied them afterward. At the state level these methods succeeded reasonably well. In 1894, however, the strike of the American Railway Union against the Pullman Company brought the federal courts into the injunction controversy and forced Gompers to a third option, lobbying for legislative relief.

The American Railway Union struck the Pullman Palace Car Company in May, 1894. The Pullman Company operated sleeping cars on most American railroads. Its proprietor, George Pullman, was a self-made man who parlayed a stake made selling groceries to Colorado gold miners into a fortune. Pullman himself was, to labor at least, a nasty piece of work, an individualist who combined the worst features of the nineteenth-century robber baron and the medieval seigneur. Andrew Carnegie, a sharp dealer in his own right, called Pullman "a lion" and a "consummate man of affairs." Gompers described Pullman as "the most consummate type of avaricious wealth absorber, tyrant, and hypocrite." Pullman's construction and repair shops were located at, modestly enough, Pullman, Illinois. Around his works Pullman built a "model community" of houses and stores for his workers.

In reality, the model community resembled the tenement houses owned and operated by sweatshop cigar manufacturers in New York and served equally well to keep the workers in peonage. As the depression of 1893 deepened, Pullman cut his employees' wages 22 percent without at the same time reducing rents or prices in the company store. Eight months later he rejected contemptuously his workers' petition for restoration of wages or cuts in prices and fired those who presented it. It was all his property, he said, and he could do with it as he liked, leaving little doubt that he thought that the employees belonged to him as well.

The workers retaliated by going on strike. A month later, the American Railway Union held its annual convention in Chicago. The Pullman employees appealed to their fellow ARU members for help. The ARU's president, Eugene Debs, asked Pullman to submit the dispute to arbitration. Pullman declined to treat with outsiders on matters regarding his property. Had the dispute remained confined to the Pullman works, the outcome might have been different, but the ARU members, disregarding Debs's advice, refused to handle Pullman cars on the trains they worked. The boycott spread swiftly across the country and converted what had been a narrow dispute with a proprietor into a nationwide conflict with America's most powerful and thoroughly bureaucratized industry. The railroads, suffering heavily from the depression, were in no condition to suffer a disruption of business. They struck back savagely, inducing a tame judge to issue a sweeping injunction under the Sherman Act, and with the help of Attorney General Richard Olney, a railroad lawyer, persuaded President Cleveland to send troops to protect the mails. Violence broke out; Cleveland poured in more troops. More violence, violently suppressed. The strike was broken. Debs was arrested on a charge of contempt of court, appealed on the grounds that the court had no right to issue such an injunction, lost his appeal in the Supreme Court, and went to jail.

Gompers kept the AF of L clear of the immediate effects of the Pullman strike. He resisted all appeals to support the ARU, not only from Debs himself, but also from affiliate organizations such as the Chicago Federation of Labor and from John Lennon, the treasurer of the AF of L. Gompers opposed the ARU on several grounds. It had not affiliated with the AF of L. It was an industrial union, "a second edition of the K. of L. [Knights of Labor] except that they propose to confine themselves to the railroad men." It was a dual union (but not one of Gompers's making) to the railroad-operating brotherhoods, which called themselves "fraternal bodies" and "mutual aid societies," denied being unions at all, accepted no unskilled members, generally opposed strikes, and frequently scabbed against one another on the rare occasions when walkouts did take place. They had been around since the 1850s, regarded the AF of L as a parvenu, and refused to affiliate with it. Gompers, nevertheless, truckled to them. The brotherhoods were old, large craft unions and potentially powerful additions to the AF of L. Gompers viewed the ARU's defeat as a victory for the brotherhoods. Keeping the federation out of the dispute, he wrote, "was the biggest service that could have been performed to maintain the integrity of the Railroad Brotherhoods. Large numbers of their members had left their organizations and joined the ARU. It meant, if not disruption, weakening [the brotherhoods] to a very serious extent."

Finally, Gompers steered clear of the fracas because he regarded it as another lost cause, the wrong fight by the wrong people at the wrong time against the wrong opponent. Even worse, it involved the kind of violence that turned the public against labor and damaged the respectable image that Gompers and the AF of L tried to project. During the strike, Gompers regarded Debs as an enemy and treated him accordingly. Afterwards, Gompers converted Debs into one of labor's martyrs, suffering for a principle vital to all laboring men. "The corporations now have their claws ready to fasten them upon the body of Debs," he cried. "Not simply to try to crush him, but they hope to awe the men of labor into silence and slavish submission. Debs must be defended and ably defended. In his person at this time he represents the Rights of labor before the law to organize, to quit work in defense, protection, and advancement of its interests."

Indeed, but the cause was lost. Gompers kept the AF of L clear of the Pullman strike, but he could not avoid its consequences. When the Supreme Court upheld the Pullman injunction, it opened the gates of the federal courts to employers who wanted to deprive trade unions of the fundamental rights necessary to their effectiveness. In 1897 the Supreme Court added to the potency of the weapon by declaring that injunctions need not be served to specific persons, but could be issued as "blanket injunctions" against certain acts by anyone.

Not all employers availed themselves of this new weapon. Most corporations preferred the simple union-smashing tactics practiced by Frick. Small employers often found it simpler and cheaper to deal with unions and stay out of the courts. Among the latter group, however, a number seized upon the injunction as a godsend. From 1902 on, Gompers and the federation were under continuous legal attack, and the cases that had the most devastating effect on the AF of L were brought not by corporate giants of the new age, but by small employers in trades as anachronistic as the craft unions they set out to destroy.

The first case in the series was that of the *Danbury Hatters.* The United Hatters of America had carried on a highly successful campaign to organize the industry, which consisted almost entirely of small, proprietor-operated factories. The Hatters' chief weapon, the boycott, proved extremely effective until they encountered D. H. Loewe of Danbury, Massachusetts. Loewe fought back; the union declared a strike. Loewe obtained an injunction under the Sherman Act and sued the striking hatters for $240,000 under Section 7, which provided for triple damages against violators. The union argued that the Sherman Act was inapplicable, but lost. The case wound its way through the courts until it reached the Supreme Court in 1908. The decision had deadly implications for trade unions because it ruled unequivocally that the Sherman Act applied to trade unions and suggested that any act of a labor organization aimed at raising wages, shortening hours, or improving working conditions could be construed as restraint of trade.

In 1906, while the *Danbury Hatters* case was still under litigation, another, the *Bucks Stove* case, got under way. This one involved Gompers personally. His defeat was the crowning achievement of an antiunion campaign launched by small employers around the turn of the century. Gompers often talked of the need for labor organizations to adapt themselves to the problems posed by the "new industrial combinations." "I had foreseen the necessity," he said, "for paralleling in the labor movement the centralization that was taking place within industrial organization." He never found a way to do this. On the other hand, he overlooked the possibility that the rise of the AF of L might generate similar reflections among the small employers with whom trade unions most often negotiated. The AF of L's growth brought increasing pressures on these employers, and they organized themselves the better to resist. They too suffered from the depression and were as frightened by the new giant corporations as were trade unions. Small operators also fell victims to discriminatory railroad rates. Seeing themselves as caretakers of a great American tradition of thrift, property, enterprise, and mobility, they reacted energetically to their declining status, calling for antitrust laws and for railroad regulation. Their efforts brought few effective results, but against trade unions they had better luck.

In cities across the country, small businessmen organized trade and employers' associations that carried out open-shop campaigns. Citing the traditional rights of property owners and of employers and workers to contract with each other without outside interference, these associations reversed the small employers' longstanding policy of accepting unions among their workers and of bargaining with them. They aped the corporate managers' methods, declining to recognize unions as bargaining agents and firing workers unless they agreed to sign "yellow-dog contracts," that is, agreements to stay out of unions as a condition of continued employment. In Dayton, Ohio, such a campaign reduced union membership by 85 percent. Similar results were obtained in other localities.

In 1903, the National Association of Manufacturers

mounted an antiunion drive on a national scale. The NAM was not, as the name might suggest, an organization of corporate moguls; it was, rather, a small businessmen's group, a kind of antilabor chamber of commerce and Lions Club combined. Decrying the closed shop (a shop that hired only union members) as un-American, the NAM attacked in industry after industry and inflicted major defeats on the building trades', meat cutters', and teamsters' unions. Not content with these tactics, the NAM decided to use the legal weapons unleashed by the Pullman case. James Van Cleve, president of the Bucks Stove and Range Company of Saint Louis and of the National Association of Manufacturers, ordered members of the stove polishers' union to work a ten-hour day instead of their accustomed nine hours. The stove polishers went on strike, declared a boycott of Van Cleve's products, and asked the federation to put Van Cleve's company on the "We Don't Patronize" list published regularly in the *American Federationist*. After some hesitation, Gompers agreed. In addition, Gompers sent circulars to all affiliates, asking their members to publicize the boycott.

Van Cleve responded by obtaining an injunction in the Supreme Court of the District of Columbia. The order forbade the AF of L and its officers to interfere with the sale of Bucks Stove's products "in any manner," including "declaring or threatening any boycott . . . or in any manner assisting such boycott." Gompers then decided to make the Bucks injunction a test case, "as it contained practically every phase of the abuse we wished to remedy." Accordingly, he defied this injunction as he had so many before. The federal court, however, did not view such cavalier behavior with the indulgence shown by many state tribunals. Gompers and two other AF of L officers were cited for contempt. Gompers received a one-year sentence. Once again the appeals dragged on. In the midst of them Van Cleve died, and his successor asked that the case against Gompers be dropped. Although Sam thus avoided a term in jail, the case inflicted another stinging defeat on the federation because it sustained the use of the injunction against an established union practice.

As a result of the combination of corporate intransigence and the counterattack by small employers, the AF of L's growth leveled off in 1904. Shorn of its cherished weapons of direct economic action, the federation faced a bleak future unless it could find a way to strike back. Not only did there seem little hope for further expansion, but the existing organization might also be wiped out. By 1902 Gompers had gone over almost entirely to the defensive. The defeats in the steel industry in 1892 and in 1901, together with the *Danbury Hatters* and the *Bucks Stove* cases, persuaded him to seek new methods to deal with both classes of employers. His strategies, coupled with his iron will and tireless energies, preserved the organization he built, but like him, the AF of L passed into cautious middle age.

IX

Politics,
Victory, and War
1906–1917

IN THE EARLY twentieth century Gompers had to redirect his energies. For years he had focused on expanding the AF of L and its effectiveness. Now its very life was at stake, threatened with extinction at the hands of its enemies — business large and small and its allies, the courts. Since direct economic action was a feeble weapon against the new industrial combinations, he tried, through sweet reason, to persuade big corporations that recognizing trade unions was in business's best interests. This tactic, however, yielded little more than his legal duels with small business and with its creature, the National Association of Manufacturers.

Rebuffed in the courts, at the bargaining table, and on the picket line, Gompers concluded he had to seek legislative relief. Reversing his previous course, he led the AF of L into politics. But, as in all things, he followed a plan based on keeping the federation an independent power, free to reward its friends and punish its enemies, regardless of party affiliation. He initiated a lobbying campaign to secure for trade unions an exemption from the Sherman Act and threw the federation's resources into the 1906 congressional election in an effort to unseat some of labor's most outspoken enemies.

These moves inaugurated a political drive that achieved its crowning victories in the passage of the Clayton Antitrust Act of 1913 and in the reelection of Woodrow Wilson in 1916. Throughout the long struggle, Gompers showed his willingness to change policies in pursuit of an unchanging goal, the preservation of the trade-union movement and his position at the head of it. In that aim he succeeded, but the cost was high, for he abandoned his campaign to organize the unskilled. The AF of L thus cut itself off from its greatest potential source of economic and political power. Tethered to its craft-union philosophy, battered by antiunion onslaughts, caged by legal bars, the AF of L found itself an increasingly irrelevant anachronism to most of American labor. Gompers had envisioned the federation as a pacemaker in the van of progress. Instead, it trailed America's march into progressivism in politics, industrialization in economy, and urbanization in society.

Gompers's chief ally in trying to reason with big business was the National Civic Federation, founded in 1900. The NCF tried to bring together representatives of the public, labor, and business. The Civic Federation acted as an agency of conciliation to head off strikes before they occurred or to settle them amicably when they took place. Although the group claimed to represent many segments of American society, in practice it drew its membership from small subsets. The public delegates tended to be clergymen and judges and played an insignificant role. The heavy work was done by the labor participants, who from the outset were limited to AF of L potentates, including Gompers, the responsible spokesman.

The business interest in the Civic Federation came from an equally narrow elite, the few powerful capitalists who preferred peaceful negotiations to all-out war. Prominent among them were Mark Hanna, Cleveland industrialist and Republican kingmaker, and August Belmont, a Wall Street financier, who represented in the big business community a strand that thought placating rather than antagonizing the workers was more profitable in the long run. As Hanna tartly put it, "An owner who won't meet his men half way is a god damned fool."

The National Civic Federation advocated the original Carnegie method — accept unions and deal with them. Until the Wagner Act of 1935 made such recognition mandatory, few large firms chose it voluntarily, and the AF of L had little luck in forcing the issue through strikes and boycotts. An alternative peaceful approach was to give enough ground on wages, hours, and working conditions to remove the workers' incentive to unionize. This method became popular in the 1920s under the euphemism "welfare capitalism."

In 1900, however, the future of industrial relations between the new giant combinations and their employees was unclear. But Hanna and a few others perceived that cooling the conflict between capital and labor offered solid advantages to business. Strikes, after all, cost money, disrupted production, shattered delivery schedules, and scattered work forces. Regrouping and retraining a labor force was wasteful. Such huge firms as United States Steel could not easily afford these losses. The bigger the firm grew, the greater was the pressure to keep its capital assets employed full time and at full capacity so as to pay bond interest and stock dividends. Labor strife could therefore have fatal results even to large firms. Carnegie Steel snapped up the new Homestead works at a bargain price from its disgruntled owners, who were persuaded by endless industrial disputes that there was no hope of an adequate return on their expensive investment. Carnegie at once made peace with the workers and profits from the plant.

The very creation of industrial combinations sometimes heightened pressure to produce, for often their stocks and bonds had a total paper value much greater than the real value of the firm's assets. For example, one of J. P. Morgan's companies, National Tube, issued $80 million worth of stock but had real assets worth only $19 million — a small hull to carry so much sail. Promoters like Morgan who assembled these paper concerns counted on their power to control markets and prices to dry out watery securities. Market and price control, however, were meaningless unless production could continue with few interruptions. To Hanna and his ilk this meant, among other things, avoiding labor disputes.

In addition to being expensive, strikes were messy. The chaos that attended them grated on the sensibilities of an age that made order a fetish. The passion for order took many forms, ranging from the standardization of threads on nuts and bolts to the mania for efficiency that sanctified time-and-motion-study cultists like Frederick Taylor. It also added a powerful psychological impetus to the basic economic motives that produced trusts and other business mergers. The thrust for order was so powerful, in fact, that it resulted in business combinations in industries where such organizations violated economic common sense. Trusts worked well enough in farm machinery and petroleum; in pickles and twine they collapsed. But to some of the capitalists who wanted to inject rational methods throughout the economy, it made sense to bring business combinations and trade unions together on the large ground of their common interests. As Gompers phrased it, "There is in our time . . . certainly a community of interests, to the end that industrial peace shall be maintained."

Another incentive for the capitalists who supported the Civic Federation was their fear of the social and political consequences of violent labor confrontations like Homestead. Such clashes ravaged the unions all right, but repeated use of Pinkertons, police, and troops might alienate the workers, perhaps even drive them into the open arms of socialists, anarchists, and other "un-American" radicals. For men like Hanna, who feared and despised socialism even more than did Gompers (they had, after all, much more to lose), it made sense to make common cause with the AF of L, an organization steeped in traditional American values. If organized labor had threatened to destroy or confiscate private property, the price of eliminating the AF of L might have been a bargain. By 1901, however, it was obvious that organized labor offered no such menace. Gompers and his troops were potential allies against the socialists, who openly advocated the elimination of private property and of capitalism. If these allies could be bought cheaply at the bargaining table, it made sense for big business to pay the small price involved.

Conciliation made another kind of political sense to the Civic Federation moguls, almost all of them Republicans. Many workers were instinctively Republicans. The GOP was still "Lincoln's party" to them, even if it was also the business-man's party. Labor strife might drive workers into a third party, or worse, into alliance with the Democrats. Hanna, for one, directly attributed the Republicans' loss of the presidency in 1892 to a public reaction against Homestead.

For his part, the Civic Federation offered several induce-ments to Gompers. It favored business recognition of unions and collective bargaining. By 1900, when he accepted the vice-presidency of the NCF, Gompers despaired of organizing the new industrial workers by the orthodox methods of the past. Nor was he certain of "holding the lines" of existing organiza-tions through direct economic action. If big business could not be brought to heel through strikes and boycotts, it could perhaps be persuaded to recognize the community of interests. He might then "see the organization of the wage earners and the organization of the employers . . . meet around the table . . . to discuss . . . the wages and hours and conditions of employment and all things consistent with [the] industrial and commercial success of our country."

Such negotiations, Gompers thought, could yield a "trade agreement," a formal recognition of standardized conditions of employment throughout an industry. Gompers's description of the trade agreement revealed his total rejection of whatever theories of class conflict he might have embraced in his mili-tant youth. It was a theoretical antithesis to Marxism. Instead of growing ineluctably more hostile to one another as Marx predicted, Gompers saw labor and capital converging. In the past he had used such terms as the "impassable chasm" between workers and owners. In 1901, he hailed "a substantial trend toward agreement between the laborers and capitalists, employed and employer, for the uninterrupted production and distribution of wealth . . . with ethical consideration for the *common interests* of all the people." Modern capitalism was moving not toward violent conflict, but toward harmony and the promotion of the general welfare. Few businessmen ever sang a sweeter capitalist song.

Converging interests and trade agreements, Gompers argued, signified the maturity of the trade-union movement and of the business system. Just as nations emerged from the endless conflicts of barbarism to make treaties recognizing one another as sovereign states worthy of respect, so too would the trade agreement serve as "a treaty between powers which recognize each other." And just as treaties meant the end of warfare as policy, so too would trade agreements end the need for union militancy. In place of strikes and boycotts would come "constructive service." Trade unions would present their constituents' needs at the bargaining table so that the natural rule of reason could operate unhampered by imperfect knowledge.

Gompers's faith in treaties as a means of averting warfare was in keeping with the mood of his times, which wished to substitute rationality for disorder. The United States had been at peace with the rest of the world since 1815, except for brief skirmishes with Mexico and Spain, conflicts that hardly counted. In the first decade of the twentieth century, the United States bustled about the world making peace in Asia and in Central and South America with treaties that seemed to stick. Besides, Gompers had nothing to lose; nothing else worked against the power of big business. If combat failed, why not try reason?

Gompers also participated in the National Civic Federation because it burnished his public image and boosted his self-esteem. Although he boasted that he "refused to meet [employers] individually or accept invitations to their homes" and that he "did not eat the food served" at NCF banquets, he obviously enjoyed consorting with such luminaries as Carnegie, Belmont, Hanna, and Vincent Astor. The Civic Federation bigwigs lionized him publicly, particularly after his 1903 denunciation of socialism. Hanna called him "Sam" and listened to his advice or at least pretended to. Gompers related with obvious relish his role in negotiating in behalf of striking blast-furnace workers at one of Hanna's steel mills. According to Sam, he exposed a practice among the mill's foremen of extorting payment from job seekers, collecting their bribes on the installment plan, then firing the workers and replacing them with new ones. Hanna discharged the culprits, saying, "Sam, I didn't know any such thing could exist in any plant and much less in a plant I owned. I am glad you brought it to my attention." Hanna then complained that although the men's cause had been just, they had presented their case "undiplomatically." "We don't raise many diplomats on . . . fifteen cents an hour," Gompers retorted. Intoxicating stuff, these chummy dealings with the man who made McKinley president.

The Civic Federation intervened in many labor disputes. It boasted that in its early years it helped settle more than a hundred strikes and failed only eighteen times. Gompers thought that the NCF's participation in the Amalgamated's strike in 1901 succeeded in that it kept a bad matter from being worse. The Amalgamated, on the other hand, thought that it had been double-crossed. Gompers's trade-union allies supported his activities by rejecting at the AF of L conventions of 1905 and 1911 resolutions condemning trade-union participation in the NCF. Some of the affiliates, however, took a harder line. In 1910, the United Mine Workers declared that no miner could hold office in the National Civic Federation. This resolution forced John Mitchell, the UMW's former president, to choose between his union and the NCF, where he headed the Trade Agreements Department. Mitchell opted for the union, but regretted "the unjust attack on the National Civic Federation which . . . has . . . consistently . . . advocate[d] industrial peace."

The socialists of course denounced Gompers's role. Some saw it as the worst kind of class collaboration – a sellout. Gompers was castigated for "reveling in aristocratic dissipation" with Belmont and others while certain labor leaders languished in jail. (He responded with sarcastic accounts of socialist conferences in Europe held in "elegant palaces" and featuring "sumptuous banquets where no workers could be seen except those who waited upon their socialist majesties" at the table.) Others thought Gompers the victim of a capitalist confidence game. Victor Berger, Milwaukee's socialist mayor, described it as a "hypocritical attempt of the [National Civic] Federation plutocrats to convince organized laboring men that the interests of capital and labor are identical." This "game" was "the shrewdest yet devised by the employers of the country," according to Morris Hillquit, a lawyer and sometime socialist theoretician. "It takes nothing from capital, it gives nothing to labor and does it all with such an appearance of generosity, that some of the guileless diplomats of labor are overwhelmed by it."

Equally enraged were the gentlemen at the other end of the spectrum, the National Association of Manufacturers. The NAM damned the Civic Federation as "an annex of the AF of L." John Kirby, head of the NAM, wrote to Seth Low, mayor of New York and a power in the NCF, that the Civic Federation's endorsement of trade unionists "and the doctrines they preach" presented "great danger to the best interests of our common country." The small businessmen who supported the NAM believed in the innate irreconcilability of workers' and employers' interests as much as did their despised enemies, the socialists. Both deplored the idea of a community of interests, the one group because they thought such harmony might hasten labor's assault on the citadel of property, the other group because they thought it might delay it.

Among corporate magnates, the NCF's attentions usually received a cold welcome. In 1902, for example, when a strike loomed in the anthracite coal fields, the NCF tried to mediate but failed. George F. Baer, president of the Reading Rail Road and spokesman for the anthracite owners, was not a man to brook interference from outsiders, especially when they worked hand in glove with union agitators. "The rights and interests of the laboring men will be protected and cared for," Baer pontificated, "not by the labor agitators, but by the Christian men to whom God in his infinite wisdom has given control of the property interests of this country." Unhappily for Gompers and for his NCF confederates, Baer, not Hanna, reflected the prevailing view of the business community. Gompers, nonetheless, remained active in the National Civic Federation, which continued to play a role in labor relations until the First World War, when it turned to other things.

As the first decade of the twentieth century passed and Gompers turned to politics, he hoped to add repeal of antitrust legislation to the "common interests" of labor and management, for many industrialists feared its potential impact on business combinations. Gompers used his NCF contacts to present his views to businessmen like Charles Flint and Samuel Colt. "I expressed myself freely and frankly, reiterating [my] statements . . . that the trust or centralized control over production was a natural development of industry and that [antitrust] legislation . . . was really a limitation on the industrial and commercial development of the United States." Gompers "favored greater freedom for employers and businessmen in the development of economic plans." He admitted that trade unions suffered most from antitrust laws and offered a bargain; he would swap union support of repeal for recognition by employers of the unions' right to organize. "Make common cause with us," he urged.

Gompers's alliance with the National Civic Federation was defensive. He hoped that the NCF's policy of recognition and bargaining would persuade the new industrial managers to abandon their search-and-destroy missions against trade unionists. He had no thought of using the NCF as an umbrella under which industrial unionism could be sheltered. Indeed, the more deeply he involved himself in the Civic Federation's affairs, the more overtly hostile he became to the industrial-union concept and the more narrowly he defined the potential scope of craft-union membership. Between 1901 and 1905 Gompers frustrated several attempts to form a national union of unskilled workers, including a union to have jurisdiction over only those laborers who could not join any existing AF of L affiliate. In 1905 he publicly reversed his previous stand favoring organization of all workers, telling a reporter for the Washington *Star* that the masses of the untrained were too dumb to be organized. Later he added that they lacked "courage," "persistence," and "vision."

He also retreated from his previous position on women. When asked by *Woman's Home Companion* in 1905 whether wives should work, he answered, "Positively and absolutely, No." "In our time," he added, "in our country . . . the wife as wage-earner is a disadvantage economically . . . and socially is unnecessary." Once he had urged the affiliates to recruit women; now he joined in forcing women out of some craft unions. He justified his actions on the grounds that industrial labor was unseemly for women and that factory employment degraded them in the name of liberty and equality.

Gompers executed yet another pirouette on racism. He discontinued his fight against Jim Crow unions and permitted craft unions to discriminate as they pleased. Contributions by Gompers to the *American Federationist* denounced black workers as unpatriotic and unwilling to make sacrifices, and chided them for being "cheap workers" who demanded "special privileges." He rejected protests lodged by Booker T.

Washington and W. E. B. Du Bois against the AF of L's policies. When the National Association for the Advancement of Colored People asked the AF of L to join it and the railroad brotherhoods in forming an interracial labor commission, Gompers ignored the appeal. When Du Bois sent Gompers a documented study of the AF of L's history of discrimination, Gompers dismissed it as "neither fair nor accurate." He declined to make specific refutations, however, saying, "I have more important work to [do] than correct 'copy' for your paper."

Toward only one component of the unskilled labor force — immigrant workers — did Gompers maintain a consistent position. He continued his campaign for restriction of immigration.

Some of Gompers's critics claimed that his abandonment of the cause of the industrial union resulted from a corrupt bargain with the business interests of the National Civic Federation. Gompers, his detractors argued, agreed not to recruit the unskilled in return for promises of recognition of his cherished trade unions and improved conditions for their members. Nothing in his career, however, suggests that he would have made such an agreement.

He was bigoted and in many ways shortsighted. Moreover, he had the quality, common to many politicians, of remaining personally incorruptible while turning a blind eye to the peccadilloes of his friends. He himself never yielded to the many temptations offered him to sell out the trade unions' interests. In fact, he seemed not tempted at all. He rejected offers to go into business; he declined political appointments with pay many times his AF of L salary. The NAM tried to bribe him; he rejected the offer and publicized it at the AF of L convention. "The Trade Union Movement means everything to me," he often said. "I love it more than I love my life." No doubt he did. Although he lived to see scandals involving rigged elections and job selling in some of the affiliates, Gompers himself remained a symbol of rectitude.

Keeping the AF of L out of industrial unionism resulted not from knavery, but from his own inflexible estimate of the trade unions' plight in the industrial age and from the pressures applied by his trusted lieutenants.

The task of unionizing the unskilled fell to the Industrial Workers of the World, the "Wobblies." The IWW emerged from a Rocky Mountain independent industrial union, the Western Federation of Miners. Starting in 1890, the WFM carried on a fifteen-year campaign of strikes and political agitation against the mine owners in the western United States. The conflict between the miners on one side and the owners, politicians, police, and militia on the other differed as much from the genteel discussions convened by the National Civic Federation as a dog fight differs from a dog show. No spirit of common interests prevailed among the hardscrabble miners and their freebooting employers. The miners, handy and quick with dynamite and firebombs, struck first and bargained later. The owners, a hard-bitten crew, responded with vigilantes, militia, lynch mobs, and strikebreakers. Dynamiting, arson, ambuscades, arrests without trial, deportations, flagrant disregard of the Constitution including the suspension of *habeas corpus* — all these and more punctuated the miners' frontier war with their employers.

Sometimes one side prevailed, sometimes the other. After a particularly brutal defeat at the aptly named town of Cripple Creek, Colorado, in 1904, the WFM decided it must find allies. Rejecting the AF of L as too eastern, too conservative, and too trade-union oriented, the WFM attracted a potpourri of characters and dissidents, including the rambunctious De Leon, the firebreathing "Mother" Jones, an organizer for the United Mine Workers, and a jambalaya of socialists and delegates from dissatisfied AF of L unions. In 1905, this odd coalition brought forth the Industrial Workers of the World. It was to be "one big union," an industrial union of all workers, organized by departments that would work together to improve labor conditions by direct action, to form a third political party, and to overthrow capitalism and establish a common-wealth of cooperatives.

This organization, put together by builders using blueprints ranging from hardheaded realism to dreamy utopianism, be-gan to fall apart as soon as it was assembled. Designed as an anaconda to crush the life out of exploiting capitalism, it proved instead to be a self-destructive worm, twisting itself into pieces, some of which died quickly, some of which squirmed impotently for a time. One segment, however, grew strong. The "real" or "Chicago" faction of the IWW, the legitimate descendant of the original group, emerged in 1908 as a forceful agency of industrial unionism.

The IWW set out to organize the unorganized and achieved impressive results against ferocious opposition. First it had to fight for the right to present its message publicly. In company towns, the local forces of law and order often forbade public demonstrations. In Spokane, Kansas City, Fresno, San Diego, and other cities, the Wobblies fought and won court battles for the right of free speech. From there they went on to support unskilled workers in the textile industry, aiding strikes against New England woolen mills in 1912 and against Paterson, New Jersey, silk mills in 1913. On the Great Plains they successfully united migratory farm labor (a chore that the AF of L and the CIO have never managed to duplicate) into the Agricultural Workers Organization, which wrung higher wages and better working conditions from notoriously tightfisted farmers in 1915. In addition, they successfully orga-nized the masses of unskilled labor in the timber and wood-products industry. The Wobblies did what Gompers and the AF of L said could not be done: they united the unskilled — women, blacks, immigrants from dozens of ethnic groups — in a common cause. They did so without the AF of L's help, and often despite its vigorous opposition.

But the Wobblies' hard-won organizations soon evaporated, casualties of the IWW's internal weakness, of their leaders' loss of popularity incurred by opposing America's participation in the First World War, and of the antiunion campaigns that followed the Armistice. Their solid achievements in civil rights and in industrial organizations were concealed by their romantic aura. Their emotional songs, their bombastic denunciations of their enemies, the beatings and lynchings they suffered, the courage and individualism of leaders like Joe Hill and Big Bill Haywood — these all became part of American folklore. The Wobblies became a legend, regarded wistfully by some and thankfully by others as the revolution that failed and lionized widely as examples of the great American tradition of the underdog.

Yet beneath the legend, the IWW's history offered a hard, practical lesson: Gompers was wrong about industrial unionism's possibilities. It could have been done despite injunctions, militia, and the whole arsenal of weapons in the hands of business. And, as the CIO demonstrated in the 1930s, it could have been done without sacrificing the trade unions to the industrial-union cause or embracing an unrealistic creed, either of revolution or of utopianism. Although the Wobblies' campaign was couched in the tough language of class warfare, their actual demands were neither radical nor revolutionary. They wanted the right to organize and to bargain; through bargaining they sought better wages and conditions. In short, the Wobblies resembled Gompers in his younger, more militant days: radical talk fronting a practical program. Had Gompers perceived this he might have found a way to tie the AF of L to the IWW's program, thereby providing industrial unionism with the experience, stability, and financial resources it lacked.

But Gompers at sixty was not the Gompers of thirty. Gone were the hard, fighter's body and the truculent, bristling mustache, replaced by the paunchy, fatherly figure with a black skullcap hiding a bald patch. He could not identify the promise of the IWW with the cause he had followed all his life. Instead, he did to them as his enemies had often done to him: he attacked their superficialities and ignored the honest purpose beneath. The IWW, he said, had a plan "too chimerical [for] an intelligent man or woman confronted with the practical problem of securing a better home, better food and clothing, and a better life." In following the IWW, he added, "unorganized and exploited workers were misled into chasing a will-o'-the-wisp."

Meanwhile, Gompers pursued a will-o'-the-wisp of his own, a political campaign to legitimize craft unions. By 1906 the implications of the *Danbury Hatters* and the *Bucks Stove* cases, the federation's stagnant membership rolls, and the National Civic Federation's limited effectiveness in blunting corporate attacks convinced Gompers that he must organize a systematic political campaign. The NAM had already entered politics, lobbying for legislation favorable to business and contributing to sympathetic candidates who ousted many trade-union incumbents in the elections of 1904.

The AF of L had maintained its own lobbyists in Washington since 1895 when it sent Strasser to the Capital along with Andrew Furuseth, a former seaman who made a lifetime crusade of improving working conditions in the shipping industry. In 1897 Gompers moved the AF of L's headquarters to Washington, where it later built its own office building, a union-made symbol of permanence and respectability that delighted Gompers. As labor's responsible spokesman, Gompers had ready access to presidents, senators, and congressmen. They flattered him with respectful treatment, but they ignored his requests for aid.

Finally out of patience in the spring of 1906, Gompers and the AF of L's executive council prepared "Labor's Bill of Grievances" and sent a copy of it to President Theodore Roosevelt as well as to all members of Congress. The Bill of Grievances demanded an effective eight-hour law, rigorously enforced, for government employees; prohibition of convict labor in private industry, restriction of immigration, and legislative relief from antitrust laws and injunctions. Failing such action, the manifesto threatened massive retaliatory participation in the fall elections. Armed with this writ, Gompers went up Capitol Hill to see the president and the congressional leaders. He found steep, rough going.

Roosevelt, who abandoned his silk-stocking airs for bullying belligerence when confronted, promised to enforce the existing eight-hour law, but brusquely dismissed the other demands as unnecessary or impossible. Uncle Joe Cannon, the powerful Speaker of the House, swore at Gompers and threw him out of his office. The antilabor big guns in the press opened fire on the AF of L's intrusion into politics, accusing it of wanting "government by intimidation," "a class Congress and a class judiciary," thereby rallying against labor the public's opposition to any "un-American" movement.

Rebuffed, Gompers and the unions prepared an assault for the fall elections. Revoking its longstanding position, the executive council urged the affiliates to enter the campaign energetically and as organizations, not as individuals. State and local unions should publicly endorse and work for candidates, regardless of party, who supported labor legislation. If neither party's candidate promised help, the unions should nominate a labor contender as a last resort. This tactic was both shrewd and realistic. It armed the AF of L with a political weapon without tying it to a specific party, thus avoiding the fate of the Knights of Labor, which had chained itself to the Populists. Moreover, Gompers knew there was no such thing as a "bloc labor vote," however much business and the press might howl. Workingmen were Americans first and workers a long way second. "Labor men," he said, "were identified with political parties and guided by the same sense of loyalty to them that influenced [most] American citizens." By urging them to back sympathetic candidates regardless of party, he hoped to marshal a political force without asking them to sacrifice their traditional independence. To coordinate this program, as well as to quiz candidates on their positions, to publicize their voting records, and to produce campaign literature, Gompers set up a labor representative committee, which he headed himself.

For his personal target Gompers chose Congressman Charles Littlefield of Maine, which held its election before the rest of the country and which was therefore regarded as a political weather vane. Littlefield had thoroughly antagonized Gompers in the past by leading the opposition to laws that would have exempted labor from the Sherman Act. He had also, like so many of Gompers's enemies over the years, incurred Sam's personal wrath by treating him rudely.

Both sides poured men and money into Maine. Against Gompers and his trade-union troops (none too numerous in bucolic Maine) the Republicans arrayed such party heavyweights as Secretary of War William Howard Taft, Senators Henry Cabot Lodge and Albert J. Beveridge, and Speaker Cannon. Newspapers stepped up their attack on labor, warning that Littlefield's defeat would lead to a "tyranny of labor interests." The NAM rallied to the Littlefield cause with campaign funds.

Gompers's entry into politics thoroughly frightened the Republican stalwarts. Roosevelt himself proclaimed that Littlefield's defeat would be a "calamity . . . for the country," and in the midst of the campaign he suddenly ordered that the eight-hour law for federal employees be applied to contractors working for the government. The Boston *Herald* observed that "Gompers seems to have got the administration on the run."

Run it might have, but fall it did not. Littlefield was reelected, though his previous majority of 5,400 in 1904 dropped to less than 1,000 in 1906. This result, added to the simultaneous reduction of the Republican congressional majority and the election of several card-carrying unionists, convinced Gompers that he was on the right track. Since, as he said, "the labor offensive of 1906 was . . . my responsibility

[and] my leadership was on trial," he interpreted the outcome of the trial favorably and looked confidently to better results in the future. The threat of labor's participation in the election of 1908, a presidential year, would, he thought, generate a more cooperative spirit on Capitol Hill. In this he deluded himself. Effectively controlled by Cannon in the House and by Nelson Aldrich in the Senate, Congress remained unresponsive, as did Roosevelt in the White House.

In 1908 Gompers fired up labor's political engine once more. The Supreme Court's devastating decision in the *Danbury Hatters* case, handed down in February, helped raise the pressure. Under a full head of steam Gompers, supported this time by farm organizations and even by the usually docile railroad brotherhoods, charged Capitol Hill once more. "Labor's Protest to Congress" demanded a curb on court interference in labor affairs, exemption from the Sherman Act, and protection of labor's freedom of speech and press. (For this last the Wobblies were simultaneously battling in the West, using the more direct method of speaking on soapboxes until the police yanked them down and jailed them.) Only quick congressional action, Gompers said, would avert a crisis. Otherwise, labor and its sympathizers would hold "the party in power . . . primarily responsible for the failure to give prompt, full and effective Congressional relief."

Relief died aborning. Cannon bottled it up in committee, a time-honored means of bogging down the democratic process, which the Speaker had elevated to a fine art. Gompers then took labor's political program to the parties' national conventions. In Chicago, the Republicans contemptuously shunted him off to a subcommittee of the platform committee. This toothless little conclave gave him ten minutes, dismissed his program, and told him, "Go to Denver" (where the Democrats were convening). Adding injury to insult the Republicans nominated the corpulent Taft for the presidency. Labor regarded Taft as a prime enemy because of his participation in the Littlefield campaign and because he had issued one of the many injunctions during the Pullman strike. Clearly, no help could be expected from the Republican quarter.

In Denver, Gompers received a more sympathetic hearing. The Democrats adopted a congenial labor plank and wheeled out the old prairie war-horse, William Jennings Bryan, for one more run at the White House. As the quadrennial presidential circus got under way, Gompers and his supporters joined the campaign for Bryan. Gompers denounced Taft as an "injunction judge." Taft bellowed about Gompers's "insidious attack on the courts." On Labor Day Gompers went to speak in Uncle Joe Cannon's hometown, Danville, Illinois. Learning that Cannon's property — banks, homes, businesses, town buildings — bounded the public square and that the Cannon-owned street railway circled it, Gompers mounted the platform and parodied "The Charge of the Light Brigade":

> Cannon in front of you,
> Cannon in back of you
> Volleyed and thundered;
> Yours not to reason why,
> Yours to vote for Cannon and die,
> You foolish six hundred!

Once again, however, the Republicans triumphed. Taft hulked into the White House, and Uncle Joe returned to his powerful post. But Gompers, master of the politician's art of finding good omens in bad news, consoled himself knowing that Indiana Democrats credited him with unseating the Republican governor. In addition, Champ Clark, a Democratic congressman from Missouri, publicly cited Gompers as a major influence on the voting of members of the House of Representatives. For Gompers these crumbs sufficed for a loaf. He pronounced the campaign "a moral victory."

In 1910 his efforts contributed to more substantial results. He persuaded the Farmers' National Union to support labor's political platform, a genuine feat of diplomacy. Once again he tramped the hustings and at last the tide turned. "One by one," he gloated, "conspicuous enemies of labor met with political misfortune." The Democrats won a majority in the House and Champ Clark, an open admirer of Gompers, became Speaker — "and a more intrepid friend of labor never occupied that position." Fifteen trade unionists were elected to Congress and one of them, William B. Wilson, former secretary-treasurer of the United Mine Workers, became chairman of the House Labor Committee.

Under Champ Clark's prodding, the House at last began to turn out legislation favorable to labor. Although such bills got nowhere — either the Republican Senate rejected them or Taft vetoed them — Gompers awaited the election of 1912 with optimism. "We are no longer journeying in the wilderness. We are no longer in the season of mere planting and hoping. We are in the harvest time." The circumstances of the election of 1912 indeed presented labor with an excellent chance to function as a political pressure group. The Republicans, whom Gompers had privately despaired of ever converting to labor's cause, split into two factions. The regulars renominated Taft. The dissident progressives nominated the head Bull Moose, Theodore Roosevelt, who burst out of a chafing retirement.

The Democrats chose Woodrow Wilson, disappointing Gompers, who wanted Champ Clark. Gompers distrusted Wilson, whose recent conversion from an antilabor hardliner might, Gompers feared, be tossed overboard after the election. By now, however, Gompers was mesmerized by national politics. The Democrats offered the main chance so he supported them in spite of his reservations. Wilson won, as did sixteen trade-union congressmen and one senator. The Democrats held a majority in both houses of Congress. Gompers at once wrote a long letter to Wilson outlining the reasons why labor should be exempted from the Sherman Act and why the issuance of injunctions should be regulated. Wilson replied graciously, saying, "I shall take [the letter] home with me and go over it very carefully indeed, for I am sure you know my disposition in matters of this kind."

Gompers ignored the fact that the letter promised only thought, not action. Moreover, the first two years of Wilson's presidency produced little substantive evidence to support Wilson's claim of sympathy for labor. Only one major bill, the Clayton Antitrust Act, became law. Gompers and the AF of L executive committee, however, thought it an enormous victory, more than enough to justify continued support of Wilson and his party. Gompers recalled sitting in the Senate gallery as the bill passed: "My emotions well-nigh overcame me." Wilson sent him the pen with which he signed the bill, and Gompers framed it proudly.

Hailing the labor clauses of the Clayton Act as "the most comprehensive and most fundamental legislation in behalf of human liberty . . . anywhere in the world," Gompers called it "labor's Magna Carta." The AF of L executive committee exulted in its political success. The Clayton Act secured "to the workers of America those fundamental principles of industrial liberty which were . . . the chief features of the 'Bill of Grievances' and were the objectives of the political policy which the American Federation of Labor inaugurated in 1906."

Gompers and his comrades fastened on the clauses of the Clayton Act that declared "that the labor of a human being is not a commodity or article of commerce. Nothing contained in the antitrust laws shall be construed to forbid the existence and operation of labor . . . organizations instituted for the purpose of mutual help . . . or to forbid or restrain individual members . . . from lawfully [ah, there's a rub!] carrying out the legitimate objects [there's another!] thereof, nor shall such organizations be [considered] illegal combinations or conspiracies in restraint of trade." These lines, Gompers felt, clearly gave trade unions the right to exist; furthermore, a favorable interpretation of the terms "lawful" and "legitimate objects" would legitimize labor's use of strikes and boycotts in pursuit of better wages and better working conditions.

He counted on the "labor is not a commodity"' clause to elicit such favorable rulings from the courts. Gompers saw this as a legalistic statement of his often repeated maxim that "you cannot weigh a human soul on the same scale as you weigh a piece of pork." Theoretically, at least, the Clayton Act distinguished between human rights and property rights. If the courts could be persuaded to accept the distinction, and to declare human rights superior, then labor might nullify the advantages gained by employers who treated labor (with the courts' acquiescence) as a commodity subject to property laws.

Wilson himself vindicated Gompers's optimism:

Justice has been done to the laborer. His labor is no longer to be regarded as . . . an inanimate object of commerce disconnected with the fortunes and happiness of a human being [and] to be dealt with as an object of sale or barter.

But that, great as it is, is hardly more than the *natural and inevitable* corollary of a law whose object is *individual freedom and initiative* as against any kind of private domination. (Italics added.)

In an address at the dedication of the AF of L office building, Wilson added:

The courts must not treat . . . a man's labor . . . as if it were a commodity, but must treat it as a part of his life. I am sorry that there were any judges in the United States who had to be told that. It is so obvious that it seems to me that that section of the Clayton Act were a return to the primer of human liberty; but if the judges have to have the primer opened before them, I am willing to open it.

The Clayton Act had other sections, however, and other pages of the "primer of liberty" told a different story. From the outset of the Act's writing there were warning signs. Many legislators, and Wilson himself, denied that the intention of the bill was to exempt labor from the Sherman Act. The Clayton Act merely protected unions against charges of conspiracy. It did not forbid injunctions against picketing and boycotts or prevent damage suits against unions. Senator Knute Nelson, a conservative Republican, called the labor clauses a sop that made unions feel that they had gained ground when in fact they had not. That the courts could find union activity unlawful under the Clayton Act was a harsh fact soon demonstrated. A series of cases from *Hitchman Coal* in 1917 to *Deering* v. *Duplex Printing* in 1921 upheld the use of injunctions and yellow-dog contracts.

In 1914, however, the Clayton Act seemed a great victory. More triumphs soon followed. The election returns of 1914, which greatly reduced the Democratic majority, convinced Wilson and his party of the public's demand for sweeping reforms. The congressional machinery picked up speed and purpose. Among its products were laws that eventually enacted virtually all of Labor's Bill of Grievances. In addition, when the post of secretary of labor was added to the cabinet in 1914, William Wilson of the United Mine Workers was named to it. This action particularly pleased Gompers, for it seemed to garb the labor movement in the mantle of respectability he had sought for so long. Now, Gompers thought, labor would have "a paramount voice" at the nation's highest council. By the time of the presidential election of 1916, labor had made enough legislative progress that Gompers, casting aside his previous doubts, saw Woodrow Wilson as a savior.

Gompers, though now sixty-six years old, threw himself into the campaign with unprecedented intensity. He denounced the Republican candidate, Charles Evans Hughes, as "the reactionary candidate of predatory wealth." Wilson he praised as a man of "clear vision and courageous heart and mind," a man dedicated to progress, justice, freedom, and humanity. "Because of that spirit and its results in definite laws and policies," he asked: "How can liberty-loving Americans loyal to the Republic and its ideals fail to sustain an Executive who has done so much for their realization?"

The public sustained Wilson all right. Shortly after the

election, the secretary to the Democratic campaign manager told Gompers that he had contributed more to Wilson's reelection than had any other individual. Gompers exulted. His policies, the creed by which he had lived, all had been vindicated. Not only had labor broken the Republican yoke and helped elect and then reelect a sympathetic president and Congress that pushed through long-sought laws, but organized labor had also achieved respectability and acceptance at the highest level of government. Adding to Gompers's joy, an increase in AF of L unions' membership had accompanied the federation's political gains. After hovering around 1.5 million after 1905, membership began to increase in 1910, the year the Democrats won a majority in the House of Representatives. By 1917 it reached 2.4 million.

In his own mind, the Old Man had succeeded, and success justified everything. His enemies, the Knights, the socialists, the Populists — all these and more had followed false trails up blind alleys. He and his faithful had known the way all along, and it carried them to the top. Small wonder he felt such pride in the past, such confidence in the future. It was truly his finest hour, and although he could not see it, it was the time of his last great triumph. Honor he deserved, but both the changing political climate and the growth of the federation's membership owed more to others than to him. The forces that powered both were nearly spent in 1917. It was to be many years before organized labor could make new gains for itself, and before then, many setbacks lay in store.

The AF of L legislative program, which traveled from conception to fruition in ten years, made such swift progress not so much because of the potency of the AF of L's political voice, but because it got caught up in the progressive reform wave that swept the country in the early twentieth century. Progressivism was complex, made up of many parts, some of them conflicting. What bound it together was a feeling, first voiced in the nineteenth century by farmers, small businessmen, and trade unionists, that freedom of enterprise had somehow resulted in huge business combinations that destroyed both the competitive economy and individual rights. By the early twentieth century, this minority protest grew to a consensus embraced by diverse interest groups in American society. The fusion of the farmers' union and the AF of L's programs exemplified the process of coalition at work.

Somehow, something had gone wrong; somehow, something had to be done. Socialism, of course, offered one answer, and it was attractive enough to bring the Socialist party its largest membership in history by 1917, to win 3.2 percent of the popular vote for its presidential candidate in 1916, and to force progressives in both major parties to borrow a few planks for their own platforms. For the overwhelming majority of Americans, however, socialism, with its revolutionary implications, held few charms. Retaining their faith in rational solutions, their commitment to private property, and their trust in the efficacy of law, Americans turned as always to the orthodox political process for reform. They wanted to tune the engine, not scrap the whole vehicle. In the economy there seemed two ways to use the government to restore the individual's rights: break up big business, or regulate it.

The regulators won and produced remedial legislation, including, among others, bills that set up agencies to control production and sales in industries like food and drugs, a law to curb railroad abuses by toughening the regulatory powers of the Interstate Commerce Commission, a measure that established the Federal Reserve banking system to stabilize the monetary system, and a barrage of laws relating to labor. All this progressive legislation had the same underlying justifications: the restoration of individual rights and the protection of the general welfare. The answer to big business was big government to help the little man catch up. There was a lot of catching up to do. As always, legislative and judicial recognition of problems lagged far behind the problems themselves.

The world, let alone the United States, had never known business combinations as powerful as United States Steel,

Standard Oil, and similar behemoths, so such firms faced few legal restraints until public opinion demanded them. Among these were controls of the abuse of labor. Progressive labor legislation included far more than just Gompers's 1906 agenda. It embraced issues he had long supported, such as child labor laws, some he had supported halfheartedly, such as workmen's compensation, and others he flatly opposed, such as regulation of hours for women. The new tide that carried through such legislation also engulfed the courts; decisions that had overturned regulatory laws as violations of individual, property, or contract rights were reversed in state and federal courts.

Gompers, then, driven by the needs of his ego, overestimated his and labor's contribution to the reform impetus; in fact, a powerful consensus throughout society drove it on. He had contributed by publicizing wrongs, by formulating some remedies, and by supporting the Democratic party. More important was his unwavering adherence to perceptions he had long before: that American workers were not a class but shared the beliefs of their fellow citizens and would support no movement that disavowed the popular creed; that big business combinations were inevitable and efficient, to be dealt with realistically not by trying to break them up; that mechanization could bring great wealth, which labor could share, and therefore should be welcomed, not opposed.

By making these perceptions the keystone of the AF of L's policy, Gompers made trade unions respectable and kept the federation in the mainstream of American values. When the tidal wave rolled, the AF of L was carried along, while more radical, less realistic groups were left on shore.

The AF of L's increase in membership, though spread across many trades, derived largely (70 percent) from drives carried out in four industries: railway shop crafts, building trades, clothing, and coal mining. The affiliates were energized not only by the political successes of the AF of L, but also by two external threats — the IWW's energetic industrial unionism and the resurgence of the socialists. The first three industries that contributed to expanding membership were organized into craft unions of the kind Gompers favored. The coal miners, however, were another matter. The United Mine Workers was an industrial union and proud of it. Much of its leadership was fractious, and sometimes openly defiant of the AF of L's hierarchs. When AF of L conventions voted on Gompers's proposals, the miners often voted no. The only man other than Gompers who ever held the federation's presidency was John McBride, a miner, who held office in 1895. The only man who subsequently mounted a serious challenge thereafter was John L. Lewis, also a miner, who got a third of the votes in 1921. Naturally enough, Gompers watched the miners' growth with suspicion, though he welcomed any addition to the federation's ranks.

Gompers deserved little credit for these organizing successes. While the affiliates canvassed the coal mines and prowled through garment district sweatshops, Sam plunged ever deeper into politics. Without him, of course, there might have been no federation to support organizers and no affiliates to send them out. For that he could rightfully be proud.

As 1917 passed, Gompers watched with satisfaction as Congress added an eight-hour law for railroad workers and a literacy test for immigrants to the statute books. Bursting with patriotism and hero worship, he followed Wilson, as the president who said he would never take America to war did just that.

X

War, Victory, and Stagnation

1917–1924

On APRIL 2, 1917, President Wilson asked Congress to declare war on Germany. Wilson said he needed war "to achieve the ultimate peace of the world and . . . the liberation of its people." So America marched off "to make the world safe for Democracy."

In the van of this crusade came Samuel Gompers. In the past he had so vehemently opposed war that the Carnegie Peace Foundation had planned to publish a volume of his pacifist utterings. This project now had to be abandoned, for Gompers's devotion to Wilson swiftly converted him from pacifist to warmonger. As Wilson put his preparedness program on the road in 1916, he called on Gompers to whip labor's troops into line. Sam responded eagerly. No longer was he an outsider. The president needed him; America needed him; the world needed him. He would not fail them. His pride, his fighting spirit, his patriotism welled up and flooded him with martial spirit.

In October, 1916, Wilson appointed Gompers to the advisory committee to the National Council of Defense. "Henceforth," one historian observed, "he became a volcano from whose crater poured forth fiery maledictions against the Kaiser and flaming slogans having to do with Democracy." Gompers himself testified to his conversion to the cause of peace through war. At a meeting of the advisory committee, he said:

Providence and opportunity have made me a leader of men who work with their hands. . . . They have accepted me as their teacher. . . . Ten million of these honest men are now looking to me for guidance and leadership in this menace to their principles, to their country, and to their homes. All around us aggression is in the air. . . . You, my associates . . . no longer believe that peaceful methods will prevail.

At that point he buried his head in his hands and wept. Then he cried:

By God's help I can no longer stand it! I must yield. War to suppress crime is justifiable; and with all my energy and influence I will induce my boys, many of them already straining at the leash, to follow me.

Not all the boys, however, were straining at the leash. The AF òf L had on record a long series of resolutions against war, and much of the trade-unions' leadership was loath to repudiate them. Time and again, Gompers summoned the clans and battered away at them, appealing to their patriotism and damning dissenters as "treasonable to the government of the United States" and "disloyal to the American Federation of Labor." In this hortatory role, one of his biographers said, he "presented a curious figure. Here was a Dutch Jew, born in England, turned violently American, leading cohorts of Irishmen to make the world safe for Democracy."

The crusading spirit prevailed. As the crucible of war heated up, the American fighting blood, always at the simmer, rose to a boil. Pacifism melted away. For Americans the war offered a chance too good to miss: an opportunity to see the world; to break the boredom of life in factories and on farms by getting into a good fight; to straighten up the world's affairs after the Europeans had made a mess of them; to march through streets strewn with roses and lined with cheering crowds of notoriously loose and reputedly inventive French women. All this and a chance to make the world safe for democracy too. In the end, most of the boys marched off willingly enough.

At home, Gompers turned propagandist. With his acid tongue and pen he rained abuse on pacifists, many of whom, conveniently enough, were in the ranks of his old archenemies, the socialists. Through his contacts in European labor circles, he tried to lash new life into the flagging Allies. He never became so carried away, however, as to overlook the practical advantages of war. Not all the labor force was going to France; Sam drove a hard bargain for those who stayed behind. The country needed industrial peace at home to fight its mechanized war abroad. Wartime labor relations were made the province of the War Labor Board, and Sam saw to it that the board's principles included several dear to labor. There were to be no strikes by labor or lockouts by employers; the right of collective bargaining was recognized, as was the right to organize. Other guidelines included the eight-hour day and equal pay for women.

The War Labor Board heard 1,250 cases and generally arranged settlements favorable to labor. It did so not only out of a desire to keep the guns and ammunition flowing, but also because the wartime economy made such settlements relatively painless. There was money enough for all. Demand for goods ran high; the supply of labor, diminished by the four million men in the armed forces and by the wartime interruption to immigration, ran low. In these propitious conditions the AF of L grew steadily from 2.4 million on January 1, 1917, to 3.3 million on January 1, 1919.

Finally, in November, 1918, the savage Hun, having made the mistake of taking on the rest of the industrialized world, gave up the fight. The boys, or most of them, came marching home. Sam thought his dedicated service entitled him to a junket to Versailles on the Peace Commission, but he had to settle for leading the United States delegation to the International Labor Organization. Bitterly disappointed in his internationalist ambitions, he nevertheless shared the jubilation that prevailed in the AF of L at the war's end. The past two years had produced "unshakable" gains for labor, or so the AF of L's potentates thought. From its new position of strength, the federation hoped to advance with a program of "reconstruction," including permanent recognition for such wartime expedients as the right to organize, shorter hours, and equal pay for women. It also advocated a broad legislative program featuring the abolition of child labor, drastic limitations on immigration, stronger workmen's compensation laws, and public ownership of utilities. An energetic campaign for membership was to accompany this ambitious political assault.

Things went well for a while. The postwar demand for consumer goods, especially automobiles, kept the economy booming. Much of the legislative slate — immigration laws, child labor laws, workmen's compensation laws — was enacted. Union membership reached four million on January 1, 1920. For the postwar AF of L, however, the essential struggle remained what it had been since the federation's founding; it needed legal recognition of its fundamental activities: organizing, bargaining, conducting strikes and boycotts. Its hope for survival as an effective force, let alone its hope for growth, depended on such recognition, and this it could not achieve, even in the heady atmosphere that prevailed immediately after the war.

In fact, the postwar tide, which the AF of L expected to ride to new heights, soon turned. The most important wartime gains ebbed away and washed up farther out of reach than ever. Prosperity gave way to recession; jubilation in democracy's victory faded into the "Red Scare" paranoia provoked by the threat of bolshevism. A new mood of hostility replaced wartime tolerance of organized labor. Employers large and small renewed their attacks on unions. The courts nullified the Clayton Act's labor provisions; injunctions and yellow-dog contracts proliferated. Labor assaulted the steel industry once more; it suffered yet another devastating defeat. Welfare capitalism sapped labor's appeal to workers.

Under this combined assault, the federation's membership dwindled: from 4 million in 1920 to 2.9 million in 1924. Organized labor passed from the heights of its wartime power and hopes into the depths of impotence and despair, into what one historian accurately called "The Lean Years."

Gompers could muster no defense. Old, tired, nearly blind, bitterly disappointed, tethered to an obsolete strategy, he could do no more than hold on to his position and hope for the best, chanting the old formulas and snapping at enemies who came within range.

His behavior in the postwar years showed how thoroughly his once militant determination to organize all American workers had given way to an obsession with the survival of his cherished craft unions and the preservation of his own reputation. Although appointed chairman of the organizing committee for the 1919 steel strike, Gompers did little to push the drive forward. He missed meetings, declined to use his influence to rally craft unions to the steel workers' cause, went abroad in the midst of the organizing drive, and resigned from the committee on the eve of the strike. Despite Gompers's inactivity, the campaign met with an overwhelming response among the steel workers: 340,000 of them — two-thirds of the industry's work force — signed up.

The campaign and the strike that followed it frightened the steel industry, the public, and Gompers. The industry, with government help, fought back violently, breaking up union meetings and picket lines, beating, shooting, and arresting strikers (twenty-two of whom were killed) ; calling in special deputies, labor spies, and strikebreakers; and mounting a propaganda campaign that branded the strike as an attempt to bolshevize American labor. The public, already sensitized by the Red Scare, responded fearfully to the industry's alarms. Those alarms were widely publicized in the antilabor press, which capitalized on the fact that the principal strike leader, William Z. Foster, had a record as a labor radical in the IWW and that thousands of strikers were European immigrants. In such an atmosphere, the public readily sanctioned the brutal suppression of the rights of assembly, speech, and organization that contributed to the strike's collapse.

Gompers did nothing to aid the cause. Once he might have seen a great opportunity for the AF of L; now he saw only a threat to its existence and his preeminence. Fearful that the combined force of business and government, backed by the public, might identify the craft unions with the steel workers and crush them both, Gompers disassociated himself from the whole affair. He defended his conduct on the grounds that the strikers had disregarded his cautionary advice and that Foster was an unreconstructed radical using the steel dispute as a Trojan Horse to spirit his ideas into the AF of L's citadel. Gompers also feared that victory in the steel strike would shift the labor movement's center of power toward the unskilled workers and their militant champions and away from skilled tradesmen and the AF of L's aging, conservative leaders. His coterie of supporters so obviously shared this apprehension that United States Attorney General J. Mitchell Palmer, chief witch hunter during the Red Scare, described the defeat of the steel strike as "a complete victory for the American Federation of Labor."

Gompers also used the Red Scare as a weapon against his opponents within the AF of L. The antibolshevik hysteria took care of his old enemies, the socialists. When new foes, led by John L. Lewis of the United Mine Workers, appeared in the younger ranks demanding industrial unionism, Gompers and his lieutenants tarred the upstarts with the red brush by denouncing them as communist-inspired and threw them to the witch hunters.

With such tactics and the aid of his aged colleagues, Gompers remained at the head of the AF of L. He had become the "Great Totem" of labor, more its symbol than its leader.

When labor's cooperation was sought, as during the war, "Mr. Gompers" was trundled out as the venerable emblem of respectable workers. When he had served his purpose, "Sam" was unceremoniously shoved offstage, as when he was excluded from the peace negotiations.

Hoping to find abroad the respect and adulation he felt denied at home, Gompers squandered his dwindling strength in the postwar years, promoting labor organizations in countries like Mexico and pursuing his old dream of an international federation of unions. His involvement in the Pan American Federation of Labor, the International Labor Organization, and similar convocations brought him publicity, medals, and opportunities for globe-trotting. But it produced few real benefits for workers anywhere, and it allowed organized labor to become an arm — albeit a feeble one — of American foreign policy.

In a final, desperate attempt to restore momentum to his movement, Gompers endorsed Robert La Follette's 1924 presidential campaign. As the Progressive party's candidate, La Follette, as Gompers well knew, headed a lost cause. Abandoning his long-held opposition to alliances with third parties, Gompers revealed the depths of his frustration and played his last card in a losing hand.

In 1924 he died, his hand clasped in a Masonic grip by James Duncan of the granite cutters' union, one of his oldest and most trusted aides. "Say to the workers of America that I have kept the faith," he whispered as he died. Indeed he had. Tenaciously he clung to his faith in America and its creeds and in trade unions pure and simple. He had much to be proud of: the AF of L had survived its trials and clung to life despite its enemies inside and out. Skilled workers had raised their wages, shortened their hours, and through a combination of negotiation and legislation, had improved their working conditions. Led by Gompers, though belatedly, the AF of L had learned that it must apply its pressure to the vital fulcrum of American power, politics.

There were many failures as well. The AF of L did little for the great majority of American workers. By excluding the unskilled, the federation found itself a peripheral element in the American industrial economy. When Gompers died, the AF of L remained largely what it had been at birth: a federation of craft unions enrolling skilled tradesmen in old industries, most of them working in small shops. The new industrial labor force in steel, automobiles, rubber, and other industries remained unskilled and unorganized. But worse yet, the AF of L minimized its potential political power by excluding these millions of workers, whose votes the federation badly needed. Without this strength, the federation never mustered enough political clout to force the laws it needed. The AF of L's world became, as Gompers had feared, "a narrow cage," barred by injunctions, lawsuits, and yellow-dog contracts. Not until the New Deal's Wagner Act did labor achieve its Magna Carta. When it did come at last, it came less as a result of labor's influence than as a part of the torrent of legislation poured out to combat the Great Depression.

Under the Wagner Act, John L. Lewis and other leaders who built the industrial unions of the CIO did so in defiance of Gompers's heirs, who clung to the Old Man's philosophy as tightly as they held onto the leadership of the AF of L. Although the CIO's founders rejected the craft-union concept as irrelevant and obsolete, like Gompers they built an organization rooted in traditional American principles, not in class consciousness. The CIO, like the AF of L before it, exerted a conservative force, embracing the rights of property, the rule of law, and the traditions of mobility and individualism. Working people in America remain what they have always been: Americans first and workers second. For one thing, then, Gompers cannot be faulted — his unwillingness to lead "the toilers" toward revolution; they would not have followed him there.

So, in 1924, at the age of seventy-four, the Old Man died. The wheel-horse of American labor, he died in harness, still pulling. Feebly perhaps, and in the wrong direction, but with all his remaining strength. Together he and his team had dragged American trade unions from the sands of uncertainty to the rock of permanence. Having chosen his course, he followed it with all his heart, but in blinkers and far too long, straining toward the dreams of his youth. In this, Sam Gompers, so dedicated to being American, showed the most American trait of them all.

A Note on the Sources

MATERIALS ABOUND for the study of the American labor movement and Samuel Gompers. Unhappily, as the historian Gerald Stearn has observed, "the literature . . . is vast, technical, and usually dull." Much of it has been openly partisan as well, its objectivity overridden by the authors' desire to mount an attack on, or a defense of, American unions and their leaders. The attitudes of working people figured largely in the failure of socialism and other movements in the United States; therefore, these attitudes and the factors that shaped them, including the trade-union movement, demand attention and have received it, with results that often reflect the authors' sentiments toward capitalist society more accurately than they describe and explain the outlook of the workers. As the salient figure among American trade-union leaders, Gompers has naturally suffered close attention from both friends and foes. In recent years the resurgence of conflict-oriented history has, logically enough, resulted in an increased interest in labor's past that has swollen the volume of literature without, in my opinion, improving its quality. If anything, recent studies have been even more partisan than their predecessors. All must be used with care.

The primary source materials must also be approached with caution. The public writings and statements of labor leaders were obviously shaped to defend labor's position and to burnish its image in a society instinctively hostile during most of the AF of L's first half-century. Their private correspondence manifests the political maneuvering necessary to deal with a variegated and often contentious constituency.

The Gompers primary sources consist of a body of private and public writings. Foremost among the former are the Gompers Letterbooks in the AFL–CIO Library in Washington, D.C., and the Gompers Collection at the Wisconsin State Historical Society in Madison. Both have been extensively examined in the past and contain few factual surprises. They do show, however, the vast correspondence Gompers carried on during his career, and exhibit a consistency of rhetorical style in the private and the public man. Gompers wrote and spoke in a style that was stilted, awkward, and malapropos, yet often managed to be forceful at the same time.

These qualities permeate his public writings, which also exist in impressive quantities. His autobiography, *Seventy Years of Life and Labor* (New York, 1924), provides an indispensable starting point but has many limitations. Published shortly after his death, it is defensive, self-serving, often erroneous, and was filtered through his secretary, Florence Thorne, a dedicated but adulating amanuensis more concerned with her hero's image than with historical accuracy.

Gompers's views on major issues can be found in the *American Federationist* (1895–1924), and in a mass of books and pamphlets including *What Does Labor Want?* (New York, 1893), *Organized Labor, Its Struggles, Its Enemies, and Fool Friends* (Washington, D.C., 1904), *The Workers and the Eight-Hour Day* (Washington, D.C., 1915), *Labor and the War* (New York, 1919), *Labor and the Employer* (New York, 1920), and many, many more. Gompers also wrote often for magazines; for example, "The Lesson of the Recent Strikes," *North American Review*, CLIX (August, 1894), 201–206, and "Strikes and the Coal-Miners," *Forum*, XXIV (September, 1897), 27–33.

Government agencies and committees often called on Gompers for testimony, and many of these question-and-answer sessions have been conveniently collected in *The Double Edge of Labor's Sword* (Chicago, 1914).

Secondary materials for the study of Gompers's life begin with several biographies, all of them flawed. Rowland H. Harvey's *Samuel Gompers: Champion of the Toiling Masses* (Stanford, California, 1935), is great fun to read because of its vigorous, ironic prose, but is unoriginal in sources and marred by Harvey's tendency to explain history in terms of ethnic idiosyncrasies. Bernard Mandel, a charter member of the "Waiting for Lefty" school of labor history, disliked Gompers intensely, and his *Samuel Gompers* (Yellow Springs, Ohio, 1963) shows it, though the book is valuable for its scope and detailed research. Other works, such as Florence Thorne, *Samuel Gompers—American Statesman* (New York, 1957), have little value except to show the degree of hero worship Gompers induced among many of his associates.

Gompers has also been the subject of a multitude of studies that focused on some particular aspect of his life, his policies, and those of the AF of L. Among these are Louis S. Reed, *The Labor Philosophy of Samuel Gompers* (New York, 1930), John H. M. Laslett, *Labor and the Left, 1885–1924* (New York, 1970), and Stuart B. Kaufman, *Samuel Gompers and the Origins of the American Federation of Labor, 1884–1896* (Westport, Connecticut, 1973). There are dozens more.

General histories of the American labor movement include: John R. Commons *et al., History of Labor in the United States,* 4 vols. (New York, 1918–1935), the pioneer in the field. More recent are Henry Pelling, *American Labor* (Chicago, 1960), well written and interesting for its British author's viewpoint; Philip S. Foner, *History of the Labor Movement in the United States* (New York, 1947), exhibits exhaustive research coupled to a fatiguing Marxist-Leninist outlook; Joseph G. Rayback, *A History of American Labor* (New York, 1966), is comprehensive, traditional, and valuable for its bibliography, which is updated with each new edition.

Other labor studies helpful to a Gompers biographer include Gerald N. Grob, *Workers and Utopia* (Chicago, 1969), useful for its discussion of the National Labor Union, the Knights of Labor, the AF of L, and the social context in which they functioned. Grob also includes a valuable bibliographic essay. Philip Taft's *The AF of L in the Time of Gompers* (New York, 1957) has a pro-Gompers bias, but benefits from the author's access to the Minutes of the AF of L Executive Council.

Other topics such as socialism, law, and industrialization, all fundamental to a study of Gompers and labor, have extensive literatures of their own. Three standard works are David Shannon, *The Socialist Party of America* (Chicago, 1967); Charles O. Gregory, *Labor and the Law* (New York, 1961); and Edward C. Kirkland, *Industry Comes of Age* (Chicago, 1967). Those interested in extensive excursions can also peruse the sources cited in Rayback and Kaufman, mentioned above.

Finally, I must add that my view of American workers and their outlook toward society and unions owes much to my own experiences as a member (and sometimes petty official) of labor organizations in four different industries. Such personal experiences obviously may foster a subjective attitude. I have tried to minimize this, and in doing so have been aided by the fact that the workers' sentiments I observed, and indeed shared, seemed to me consistent with, and therefore explanatory of, their behavior in the past.

Acknowledgments

ONCE AGAIN I am indebted to Oscar Handlin, who works hard, respects his authors' skills, and knows how to maximize them. Marian Ferguson provided constant encouragement and no harassment. Elizabeth Fricke supervised the thankless copy-editing with skill and precision.

My friends, as always, furnished invaluable support, and I am particularly indebted to Bob Kehoe and to Barry and Gay Curtis-Lusher for supplying places to work when I needed them, to Eleanore Hofstetter of Towson State College in Baltimore for proving herself once again the world's greatest reference librarian, and to my colleague Ken Lockridge, for bringing his genius and enthusiasm as generously to my work as to his own.

My students at the University of Michigan, surely among the most delightful groups of people anywhere, have taught me as much as I have them, and two in particular, Richard Thomas and Donald Softley, contributed ideas that found their way into this book.

All books take time and money, and for their help in supplying both I am grateful to the Horace H. Rackham Fund at the University of Michigan, to the Carnegie Foundation for World Peace, and to the National Endowment for the Humanities.

Index